BURGHCLERE SIGNALMAN

Kevin Robertson

KRB Publications

ISBN 0-9542035-0-X

To assist the reader in following the sequence of the narrative, a copy of the Train Register and Passenger Timetable are reproduced on pages 36-38.

Published by
KRB Publications
2 Denewulf Close
BISHOPS WALTHAM
Hants
SO32 1GZ

Printed by M & S Print, Hailsham (01323) 449477

Preface

This is not the story of a railway line, nor a person. Instead it is the story of one man at work on just one day of his life.

Having been fascinated by and studied the former Didcot, Newbury and Southampton Railway for many years now, I have been fortunate to have had the opportunity to speak to and gather reminiscences from numerous staff—and including many of those mentioned within the text. Bill Hiscock was always a favourite. A gentle man, and who despite personal difficulty was ever willing to welcome me into his home to recount the stories of his working life at Burghclere and particularly as a signalman. Sadly he passed away some years ago and it was only some time after this, that part of a former train register from Burghclere Signal Box came into my possession. Within the worn pages of this unique document were recounted the days at work he and his colleagues would spent signalling trains through their station.

It was a small step then to use this as the basis for a description of perhaps a typical days work and which has been recounted as accurately as possible.

As such it is possible to recount a way of life that was typical on many of the former cross—country routes of the GWR, the MSWJ, Taunton to Barnstaple, Banbury—Cheltenham lines no doubt all very similar. Like the DN & S, none of these exist today and so a way of life that had survived for several generations is no more. A skill learned and practiced no longer required in today's technological age.

This then is the human element of railway working in the 1950's. I am not aware it has ever been recounted in this manner previously. Some assumptions and conclusions have had to be made of course, but these are both obvious and limited. The majority though is based on fact. One day in January 1958, a time when the trains still ran through Burghclere Station, and Bill Hiscock was the Early Turn Signalman.

Acknowledgements

I would be foolish to admit I was not more than a little wary in attempting to compile this text. Several times I doubted a rational for continuing, but persue the course I did and the results will, I sincerely hope, be of interest. I have also been encouraged by several friends along the way and who have added comment where necessary and deserved criticism also. Accordingly may I record my grateful thanks to Tony Goodyear, Roger Simmonds, David Abbott, Ken Alexander and George Pryer. Special thanks must also go to Jack Green, Bill's colleague for many years at Burghclere and who so willingly provided encouragement and his own valuable contributions.

I would also like to thank the many photographers whose work has been included not least of which are A.E. Brown—now I believe residing in America, and the late Peter Goulder—Burghclere was always a favourite location for him. Sadly many of the railwaymen featured in this narrative are no longer with us. Although regardless of this mention must be made of Harry Hillier, Bob Aldridge and Bert Gardner. Finally a special thanks to Barry and Nick at M & S Print for working so hard on my behalf.

Kevin Robertson 2002

BURGHCLERE (1943)

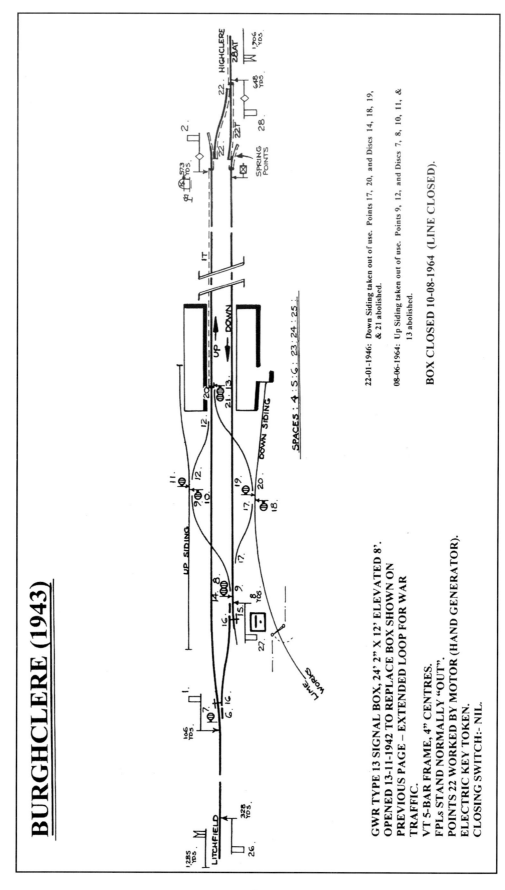

GWR TYPE 13 SIGNAL BOX, 24' 2" X 12' ELEVATED 8'.
OPENED 13-11-1942 TO REPLACE BOX SHOWN ON
PREVIOUS PAGE – EXTENDED LOOP FOR WAR
TRAFFIC.
VT 5-BAR FRAME, 4" CENTRES.
FPLs STAND NORMALLY "OUT".
POINTS 22 WORKED BY MOTOR (HAND GENERATOR).
ELECTRIC KEY TOKEN.
CLOSING SWITCH:- NIL.

22-01-1946: Down Siding taken out of use. Points 17, 20, and Discs 14, 18, 19, & 21 abolished.

08-06-1964: Up Siding taken out of use. Points 9, 12, and Discs 7, 8, 10, 11, & 13 abolished.

BOX CLOSED 10-08-1964 (LINE CLOSED).

SPACES : 4 : 5 : 6 : 23 : 24 : 25 :

Burghclere Signalman

The night air was still as Signalman Bill Hiscock turned the brass door handle of Burghclere Signal Box on the former Didcot, Newbury and Southampton Railway. Around there was no sound although in the distance the cold air carried the labouring grunt of a road lorry perhaps 2-3 miles distant on the A34 struggling up yet another of the cruel gradients on its way to the Midlands.

The noise was almost the only clue to other life, although nearer to home the various signal arms stood gaunt against the morning sky, their red lights piecing the blackness but as of yet with no trains to caution and stop.

Closing the door behind him at the same time subconsciously switching on the light, Bill mounted the steps to the operating floor. Despite years of railway work often at such inhospitable times, the cold was still noticeable, a damp clinging sensation, and reminiscent of the hours that had passed since the late turn man, Jack Green, had left nearly seven hours previously. Jack would have ensured the small pot-bellied stove was well stocked although the structure of the building - plain brick walls with the necessary openings meant it was inevitable the warmth would not last long. This could be remedied though and Bill's first task was to attend to the stove and place a kettle on top - the later an essential part of the equipment!

Next was the time-honoured tradition of signing the book, "W.C. Hiscock on duty 5/0 am. Wednesday Jan 22nd / 58" he recorded, his experienced eyes scanning the previous afternoon and evening entries for any unusual occurrences. The only item to catch his eyes being that Jack had called out his fog men, Fred Sherman and Bennie Hobbs late in the evening.

Following years of practice his eyes and mind darted around briefly noticing that Jack had left levers Nos. 16 - the south end crossover reversed, and then bolted by No. 15 which was also reversed in the frame. All the other levers stood 'normal'. At Burghclere this was normal practice to leave 16 and 15 reversed after closing and meaning there was a clear run through the station should a run-away occur elsewhere. The other advantage being that the Ganger could also run through easily with his trolley should the need arise and if he had 'occupation', although the 'box would still have to be open dur-

ing times of 'possession'. Invariably other signalman would do the same at other locations as well. Bill noticed also that the indicator for the motor points, No. 22 showed 'normal' and the various signal repeaters, 'on', lamps 'in', track circuits showing 'clear' and the clock working, its slow tick recording an almost timeless scene and which had existed at Burghclere in similar form for at least the past three generations and yet was destined to be banished forever within a further decade. Bill would also have lit his hand-lamp, probably placing it near to the stove and where the fumes from the paraffin would be sucked into the chimney. He would also leave it with the red lens showing. If a signalman needed a lamp in an emergency would invariably be to stop a train and so this would be the colour that would be needed - hence far better to be prepared.

From the record within the actual train register for 22 January 1958, the next entry shown by Bill after 'signing on' is for the first train, although it is likely this would have been preceded by the standard '5-5-5' 'Opening Signal Box' and 'Testing of Bells' to the signal boxes on either side, Woodhay to the north and Whitchurch to the south. Regretfully no train registers appear to have survived at all from the former, whilst at the latter the only known specimen covers almost the last days in 1964. It is perhaps probable however, that Bert Gardner may have been the early turn man at Woodhay and with Ken Alexander in a like role at Whitchurch and this then will be assumed for the purpose of this narrative.

Ordinarily Bill would have 'switched in' first to Woodhay and some little time after to Whitchurch. On this occasion however no sooner had Bill exchanged the necessary codes with Bert Gardner than the phone rang and his colleague was imparting the news to Bill that Control had that advised the first down service, the 1.50 am Washwood Heath to Eastleigh goods was running late - yet again. According to the timetable the train had been due to pass Woodhay at 5.17 am and Burghclere at 5.26 a.m., hence Bill's 5.00 am start time. Control though had advised Woodhay that at the moment the service had not reached Oxford and so it would be at least 60 minutes down.

Neither was this unusual for this particular service. The reason for the delay no doubt already shrouded in mystery somewhere in the Midlands area and yet destined to

Typical of the DNS in the 1950's were the freight workings, and there were several passing Burghclere on 22 January 1958. Possibly around the period No. 6363 heads south past the signal box and joins the single line no doubt bound for Eastleigh and carry Class 'C' headcodes.

Courtesy P.W. Goulder

cause difficulties to the various signalmen on the DNS south of Newbury as they wrestled to deal with a train no longer running anywhere in its booked path. Indeed a brief glance at the Burghclere Train Register for the preceding two and bit weeks since the timings of the goods had been altered to leave Birmingham at 1.50 a.m., revealed it had been upwards of an hour late on no less than 7 occasions out of the previous 14. The worst being yesterday, 21 January when it had not passed Burghclere until 7.24 a.m! Bill would also shortly impart this information to Ken at Whitchurch when he 'opened' shortly. Each signalman passing on necessary messages in this way in what were referred to as 'box-to-box' messages. When necessary, special workings such as additional trains would also be advised in like manner.

As far as 22 January was concerned, the delayed goods would not become a major problem as long as it did eventually arrive before 7.00 a.m. After this it could cause major delays to the passenger service and then Control would have to decide on the order of priorities.

Line capacity on the DNS had also been reduced since 1955 with the closure of the signal boxes at Highclere and Litchfield either side of Burghclere and so making train regulation more difficult. For the moment though any problems would be in the future and Bill occupied himself with opening to Whitchurch and immediately advising Ken of the information he had. He would also have enquired as to the progress of the Light Engine travelling from Eastleigh to Didcot and having been assured by Ken that this at least was running to time could prepare 'the road' ready for the first movement.

With his conversation over Bill picked up the duster and moved to the lever frame. Dropping the duster so that it covered the top of lever No. 15. He pulled the lever back very slightly so that he could release the catch handle. Gripping the catch handle he then pushed forward at the same time as this time also releasing the catch handle. This ensured that as soon as the lever had reached its 'normal' position back in the frame it would be held in place by the 'catch handle dog' dropping into the slot provided. Despite having been in the same position for some hours the lever moved easily. Bill expertly applying just the right amount of effort to move the rodding on the ground. With No. 15 now standing 'normal', the interlocking of the crossover was now free and he could turn his attention to No. 16. Again he adopted a similar action, one foot slightly to the right of the lever on the treads and so using his body to move the lever. Each lever also responded differently, signals requiring to be pulled but returning to 'danger' by the action of a counter-weight but levers for facing point locks and crossings needing effort in both directions. The crossover was now set for a move from the south but to complete the sequence Bill now had to pull lever No. 6 to lock the crossover for a facing direction move from Whitchurch. This was accomplished although for the present Bill left the motor points - No. 22, at the north end of the loop in their normal position as he was for now still uncertain as whether the engine would run straight through to Woodhay or be crossed with the delayed 1.50 a.m. at his station.

Years of practice had ensured that even before any of the bells had been received, Bill had ensured the 'road' was set. This would have been drummed into him as a 'strapper' a long time ago and meaning to always ensure you knew where and what the next train would be and what the next bell code you were likely to receive was. Equally important was that the points and crossings were set accordingly as were required by the clearing point. At busy locations this had perhaps more relevance, but even so the same principles applied even at sleepy Burchclere at what was by now 5.15 a.m. and so the frame showed all levers normal with the solitary exception of No. 6..

It was now a simple matter of waiting. Outside it was still dark although the ground was marginally easier to see as a light dusting of snow frozen hard after several nights of frost covered the sleepers. Peering out of the north end windows Bill could also check the oil lamps indicating the position of the token set-down and pick up posts were lit - they were, both ready to be used shortly.

Giving the stove a quick poke around, Bill may have then placed a few sheets of newspaper at the top of the stairs as an additional safeguard against bringing dirt into the signal box, before he then motioned to sit down. At their respective signal boxes all three signalmen could now relax for the present, and Bill may well have peered out onto the landscape. A few lights now visible in the former quarrymen's cottages, and indicating working men who would also soon be about their labours and which no doubt involved agriculture or estate work. In the opposite direction, the station house

that Bill had left just a short time earlier was dark and silent. No lights appearing within the booking office or waiting room as yet. In time though Bessie Sherman, the morning porter would be cycling down to the station in anticipation of the first passengers although in reality Bill knew there would be precious few of these.

Despite having prepared himself in advance the ringing of the box telephone from Ken at Whitchurch an hour later at 6.21 a.m. startled Bill. Ken was advising Bill that the engine had been put 'on-line' to him by the 'box south of Whitchurch at Sutton Scotney and could he 'offer it on' with the bells for Bill to take it or was the goods likely to arrive shortly? Bill in turn asked Bert at Woodhay for an update on the goods if he knew anything further although in reality none of this was strictly necessary for each man would have updated the next automatically should there be any relevant information. The news from Woodhay though was encouraging, Enborne Junction had just advised Bert that the 1.50. a.m. was 'about' Newbury and so would be with him shortly.

No doubt with not a little relief, Bill could now impart this to Ken and meaning that both the light engine and the goods would cross at Burghclere. With this knowledge in mind Whitchurch now officially asked Bill for the road with the requisite bell codes. One beat on the bell for 'call attention', followed by '2 pause 3' for the light engine. Bill acknowledged the codes, again using his duster to save spoiling the polished brass surface of the plunger on the token instrument. On responding to the '2 pause 3', Bill held the plunger down on the last beat noticing as he did so the galvanometer on his token instrument held over and then flicking briefly to indicate Ken had successfully obtained a token at Whitchurch. The next step was to record the time in the Train Register as 6.21 a.m. for 'Train accepted under Regulation 4'.

Ken's bell codes meant the engine would shortly be passing Whitchurch and then be put 'on-line' to Burghclere. Before this however at 6.28 a.m. came the dull thud of the gong from Woodhay. This was Bert Gardner indicating to him that the 'down' train, the 1.50. a.m. goods was 'off' Enborne Junction and he was preparing to ask Bill 'for the road'. Subconsciously perhaps, Bill flicked his duster into his hand and now walked to the Burchclere - Woodhay token machine. Again with the duster covering his palm he acknowledged the single beat at the same time noticing the galvanometer needle flicked satisfactorily. Almost immediately back came the code' '3 pause 1 pause 1'. Bill acknowledged the code holding down the plunger on the last beat until the 'galvo' again flicked to indicate that

South along the frame from No. 6 onwards. Lever frames were laid out to correspond with the actual track and signal layout, hence the down line signals were at the far end of the frame and those for the up line out of camera at the near end. In between were the levers for the various points, F.P.L.'s and ground signals. Likewise the token instrument for each section was at opposite ends of the 'box. In this view lever No. 22 - for the motor points is shown fully reversed -'R' position and the slots in the quadrant plate are also visible. The various lever plates were known as 'ivorines' and produced at Reading. Each described the movement of each lever and the 'pulls' necessary. Also to be seen is the occupation key and control instruments together with one of several lockers in which might be kept cleaning materials, paperwork, and the each man's personal items.

Courtesy; Westinghouse Brake & Signal Co.

this time Bert Gardner has successfully withdrawn a token at Woodhay. Walking then to the desk he made the necessary entry into the all-important register. The 1.50 a.m. Washwood Heath was a relatively recent introduction to the line, one of several new through freight workings that would appear in the later years and using the former DNS route as other lines were approaching line capacity.

Two minutes later at 6.30 a.m. and Ken was sending two

beats to indicate the engine was now en-route from Whitchurch. There was nothing now stopping Bill from clearing the 'up' 'home' signal, No.1 in the frame, but in practice he would not do so until the engine was within a few hundred yards of the signal. The crew seeing the signal dropping immediately ahead of them would thus recognise that they were likely to be held at the station. Again Bill made the necessary entry in the all-important Train Register.

Bill now awaited the next code and which would be two beats on the gong from Woodhay indicating the 1.50 a.m. goods was on its way south. Despite though having prepared himself in advance, the dull 'thud' of the Woodhay gong again alerted Bill. Bert was telling him that the train was entering the Woodhay – Burghclere single line section on its way south. Bill acknowledged the code back to Woodhay and walked again to the desk. Leaning across the book with his forearm he recorded the time as 6.35 a.m., possibly thinking to himself that the first passenger service in an hour or so might still yet just be unaffected. Bill could only do his best at Burghclere, he had no control over events elsewhere for no signalman liked to be responsible for delaying any train regardless as to how it was running. Again also he had a choice as to his immediate actions but this time appertaining to the 'down' home signal, No. 28. If he pulled it to 'off' the goods would have a straight run in, but now a knowledge of the gradients approaching Burghclere was useful for the train was unfitted, and meaning the only brakes were on the engine and guards van. The crew would also be attempting to run as fast as possible and it would not be appreciated by them if they passed the home signal at 'off' only to be confronted by the 'starter' a little while later at 'on'. Despite the fact that from the Woodhay direction there was a slight rise for south bound trains, Bill would have to leave the signal at danger until the light engine was safely in the loop

and thus avoiding another Whitchurch type derailment. If things went to plan the light engine would arrive and wait so as to allow the goods to have a clear run through. *(At Whitchurch in 1954 an unfitted down goods had run into the loop with the points set for the sand-drag as the signalman was expecting a passenger service from the south. The engine, unable to stop, had finished up on its side part way down the embankment and with the train piled up behind. It took a week to clear all of the debris away.)*

Moving towards the south end windows he now peered out. The cutting beyond the station restricted his view along the railway but despite this he knew that he should soon be able to see the progress of the light engine towards him by the trail of condensing steam in the cold morning air. Neither did he have long to wait, a length of pure white vapour hanging in the air perhaps some two miles away. Bill now had another choice, to allow the crew to use the token set-down point or collect the token by hand. The quicker he also could obtain the token the better, for he might manage to avoid delaying the goods. His decision then was to collect the token by hand.

With this in mind he moved to the frame collecting his duster from the desk on the way. Before he could pull the lever though he had to release the electric lock and so using one corner of the duster to cover his right palm he

A close up of the hand generator—'hurdy gurdy' provided for the motor points at Burghclere in 1942 and its associated lever No. 22. All the 'boxes from Highclere southwards on the DN & S line were fitted with these around this time and they were also to be seen on other lines as well.

Despite being of relatively modern construction there was never any water supply to the signal box and the men would bring their own or collect it from the station. Likewise stores were ordered and delivered fortnightly. These were usually brought to the 'box by Bessie—or whoever was on duty, one of the few times she would actually come to the 'box.

Courtesy; Westinghouse Brake & Signal Co.

pressed the brass release plunger on the block shelf above the lever. As he did so the sound of slight click could be heard from under the frame deep in the locking room. The remainder of the duster hung down over the shining handle of the actual lever and with his left hand Bill was able to squeeze the catch handle and pull the lever just an inch or so out of the frame. He could now release the plunger and with both hands gripping the whole of the lever he pulled back towards him. Initially this was in the same way as for the various point locks and crossovers, pulling the lever sharply but relaxing his effort as the lever nearer the fully reversed position and so allowing the catch handle to drop neatly into its slot. Again years of practice had taught him exactly how much effort would be required for each lever – all were different, and likewise if the pull was too 'springy' it would indicate a wire snag although as usual all was well. This was one signal Bill could clearly see from the box and so he quickly checked to see it had responded.

The engine would now soon be with him and so motioning towards the door he collected his coat and lamp – as he did so turning this to show a white light, and started down the stairs. Outside the dawn air was cold but still, the grey light gathering slowly above Ladle Hill behind the signal box. Standing quietly for a moment Bill thought he could just make out the sound of the 1.50. a.m. approaching from the north, his experience telling him that from the seemingly muffled sound the service was somewhere in the vicinity of Tothill on the other side of Highclere. This though was almost the only sound, by now the lorry of earlier no doubt growling its way up another incline somewhere and probably the other side of Newbury.

Bill's timing at venturing outside was also spot-on. Turning south he could see the engine was approaching him perhaps a matter of 200-300 yards distant. It passage almost silent, and somewhat surprising for a steam engine. As it drew ever closer, Bill stepped across towards the up line stopping so that he stood facing it, his white hand-lamp indicating to the crew that the signalman was standing on the ground. He then extended his right arm up and parallel to the track, the fist closed. This later behaviour was essential for safety, as the token would now easily travel up the arm as far as the elbow. To otherwise attempt to catch it between thumb and forefinger could easily result in a broken bone.

The fireman could also now be seen, leaning far and low between the cab and tender and ready to deposit the token onto Bill's outstretched arm. Bill would now remain as motionless as possible, any adjustments to

position carried out by the fireman. As the fireman expertly dropped the token onto Bill's arm accompanied by a friendly "mor'nin bobby, are we here for long……?", the engine slowly passed. Bill had been ready for the enquiry and called back, "…about five….'.

As he spoke Bill turned around to check there was a tail lamp on the tender of the 43xx, there was, the engine coming to a creaking halt on the down line just a few yards away. Bill could now return to the box, separating as he did the Whitchurch token from the carrier. On entering the box he again stamped and wiped his feet. The need might now be urgent but there was no point in creating dirt if it could be avoided. As he reached the operating floor he first hung the carrier on one of the hooks at the top of the stairs and immediately made towards the Whitchurch token instrument throwing back lever No. 1 as he passed. For signals, the plunger was only required when pulling the lever to the 'off' position and so by releasing the catch and pushing the lever gently it would return to its normal position. By looking through the window Bill could confirm the arm had responded after which he placed the token into the slot at the top of the machine and turned it through 180°. He could now guide it into one of the four slots of the machine followed by the code '2 pause 1' sent to Ken at Whitchurch to indicate the engine was clear of the section. Ken must have been waiting by the machine as it was acknowledged straight away after which Bill 'called attention' again and then sent the '3 pause 1 pause 1' to 'ask for the road' for the goods southwards. Ken again acknowledged this immediately and Bill was able to withdraw a token for the section. As he twisted it out of the slot the Whitchurch bell gave another single 'ring', this indicating to Bill that the electrical circuitry had fully responded.

In the book Bill noted the time for all three actions as 6.42 a.m., annotating the same time also for the actual time the light engine had arrived. Leaving the token for a moment lying across the open Train Register he again moved to the lever frame. Lever No. 6 was now restored to normal, No. 16 reversed and followed immediately by No.15. Locks and crossovers required a different technique in their movement and it was a question of pushing – or pulling the lever over the mid-point and then guiding it into the remainder of the way. A smooth movement was essential as a snatch could easily result in the detection not fully engaging on the ground and which would not be noticed until an attempt was later made to move the appropriate signal and then the result would be a need to 're-stroke' at least part of the route costing time and more importantly effort.

Looking south from the 'box towards the station., circa 1953, And with the down line token set down point visible. The building on the right was used by the permanent way whilst the area of ground between it and the signal box once accommodated the siding and head-shunt from the quarry. This had been taken out of use in in 1946 and probably removed shortly afterwards, hence it was not available to Bill for shunting or as a lay-by. The trailing crossover leading to the goods shed was operated by lever No. 20. The signal post and ladder dominating the left hand side of the view were No. 27—the down main starter.

Courtesy; Adrian Vaughan Collection. Box 1/91E.

By his actions then Bill had restored the frame to the state it had been in when he had arrived for duty although additionally he could now clear the signals for the down train. He did this by walking to the north end of the frame and commenced with lever No. 28, the 'down home'. As with No. 1, this signal also had a release plunger and so he adopted the same procedure to initially release the catch handle before applying the necessary force and swinging backwards. With the lever fully reversed in the frame and the noise of the mechanics subsiding Bill glanced at the red signal repeater in its brown Bakelite case on the block shelf. It too was moving, away from the 'on' swinging briefly through the centre 'wrong' area before hitting the stop on the far side with a deft click and so pointing to 'off'.

This was Bill's only indication that the signal had responded. It being too far away to visibly check the indication of the arm by sight, and besides the road bridge was in the way. (Sometimes on a cold morning it was necessary to release the wire by winding the 'derrick' a number of turns as the signal wire could contract somewhat in cold weather. The only indication this was necessary being when the lever was pulled and the electrical repeater only travelled as far as the 'wrong' indication. As such Bill would have no idea if the arm itself was almost in the clear position or may have hardly moved at all, so the solution was to restore the lever to 'normal', wind away on the 'derrick' and try again. The worse time was in summer when the wire would expand with the sun out and contract ever so rapidly as the sun went behind a cloud. As such the indication on the repeater could change with the lever fully reversed and then it was a question of hoping the arm had only just moved enough to alter the electrical contacts as 'Murphy's law' would dictate this would happen with a train close by and then to attempt to suddenly replaced the arm to 'danger' and clear it again was fraught with

Above; - One of the series of official views taken of Burghclere in the late autumn of 1942 and depicting the new works then taking place. The signal in the 'off' position is No. 1—the 'up home' whilst just beyond it can also be seen No. 7—the ground signal which allowed for 'wrong-road' movements along the 'down-main'. Alongside the track—the standard GWR 2-bolt chairs will be noted, is a single signal wire and which ran out to No. 26 the 'down advanced starter' and which was located behind the photographer. The distant signals in either direction being 'fixed'. No. 1 signal is still a wooden post, the station a mixture of both these original items and replacement tubular metal posts where a new site was required. To both sides are numerous hay-ricks, these forming much of the outward freight traffic from the station for many years. Both Bill and Jack recall long hours prior to being appointed signalmen spent heaving sheaf's onto a wagon before manhandling two heavy sheets on top. The hay would be bought by dealers during the summer but sometimes not collected until late autumn or winter and so wagon sheets could not be stored in quantity and were ordered as required. If they were wet or frozen it made the task all the more difficult. (B/Box 397/6)

Left; - Looking south towards the box and the single line on to Litchfield, Whitchurch and beyond. The new work also involved the painting of a white sighting patch on the end of the signal box and which is seen is several of the photographs. On the left the engineers wagons are stabled in the former quarry siding and which saw little use for its original purpose by this time. There is also a run-off point for the gangers trolley at right angles to the running lines. During war-time four first class coaches were stabled in the quarry sidings as an emergency provision to be used by members of parliament in the event of the bombing of Westminster. Two cleaners being despatched weekly to maintain the standard of these vehicles. Fortunately they were never needed for their intended purpose although Jack Green recounts they came in very useful for courting.....! (B/Box 397/5)

Both; GWR Official views.

risk should the driver of an approaching train mistake the restoration of a clear signal to danger in front of him as an indication that some danger had suddenly occurred ahead.)

After this it was now the turn of levers, 27 – the down starting signal, and 26 the down advanced starter neither of which were required to have release plungers. Both cleared easily, Bill able to confirm both had responded by peering out of the respective end windows. Neither was this a special effort on his part but all part of the rules and which clearly stated that the signalman should satisfy himself that the various signals and points had responded to his actions. Both Nos. 27 and 26 were also close enough to see and in the grey light of the early morn the white tell tale light from the rear on No. 27 was now obscured by its shade whilst with No. 26, and seen from the front, was showing a green light.

It never failed to intrigue Bill that the green light he saw was actually the product of blue and yellow. The oil lamp within the signal being yellow and which was then projected through blue glass to produce the green. Few of the drivers probably knew this and which was common throughout the system and yet it was something which had been pointed out to Bill when he was learning years earlier and like so many things it was well ingrained.

He now returned to the desk and collected the token. Grasping this firmly in one hand he reached for a carrier from the wall, deftly placing the token into its restraining slot as he unhurriedly made his way downstairs.

It was now a few short steps back towards the station to the token pick-up post at which point Bill mounted the ladder stopping at exactly the point where he knew he could comfortably slip the token carrier into the slot. The light engine was also still outside, the crew noticing by Bill's actions that their own wait would not be long.

Retracing his steps Bill returned to the welcoming warmth and glow of his signal box noticing as he did so the locomotive crew sat either side of their cab and drinking tea from their enamel cups. The firehole door was also open casting an orange glow back and upwards and also some warmth that would no doubt be much appreciated by the men. Entering the signal box he again stamped his feet hard on the mat to dislodge any snow. Both Bill and his colleague Jack were fastidious on cleanliness within their working environment and there was little point in making the floor unnecessarily dirty when this could be avoided.

The down service would by now be getting close, the distance from Highclere to Burghclere just a couple of miles and so Bill positioned himself by the north end of the frame his hand resting on his duster and which was draped over lever No. 28. For the moment the only sound came from the steady rhythmic ticking of the clock punctuated also by an occasional click as steam caused the lid of his kettle to rise and then fall back. Then came the first sign of movement elsewhere, track - circuit repeater No. '28 AT' clicked to 'track-occupied' and telling Bill that the goods was now within 200 yards of No. 28 signal. As with all the various instruments in the box, each made its own distinctive sound, some slow to move and others bouncing off the stop to produce a double type of click. A few seconds later track circuit '22T' moved and showing the head of the train had now entered the loop and would shortly be visible under the bridge.

Bill peered through the station towards the bridge. He did not have long to wait, a 'phut-phut' sound from the engine's vacuum pump clearly audible as a darkened shape appeared under the bridge. Encasing it at the front were several wisps of steam whilst clearly visible also was the glow from the headlamps and which seemed to dance in tune with the engine as it slowly rattled and shook its way towards him. Behind the engine would be the train but it was not possible to make this out in the gloom and likewise the only indication of its length being when track circuit '28 AT' clicked again as it returned to 'track-clear'.

To any signalman an approaching train always seemed to take an age to arrive and this one was no exception, although in practice it was the crew checking to see if the token exchange was to be by hand or by the carrier. No doubt satisfying themselves that Bill was peering from the box itself the fireman could be seen with the 'Woodhay - Burghclere' token in hand ready to deposit it on the arm after which he would immediately gather the new token for the next section to Whitchurch.

The train came ever closer, track circuit '22T' also returning to 'track clear'. As the engine nearer and then passed the signal box, Bill was able to observe the crew, the driver on the right wrapped up in great coat and leggings against the cold whilst also observing his mate leaning out ready to exchange the tokens. Rarely did they miss, Bill well aware of the language that would emanate on the footplate if the driver were forced to stop due to the incompetence of his mate at grabbing the token. Bill could not be sure they had been successful although this was confirmed as the train continued at the same pace before entering the single line again shortly

Another of the superb official views and this time of the north end of Burghclere loop and looking towards Highclere and Woodhay. The line was a down gradient in this direction—the pronounced dip visible at the end of the cutting. The hut to the left housed the auxiliary token instrument whilst to the right was the limit of shunt board as a reminder of the presence of the spring loaded catch-point just beyond. (See text in relation to the runaway horse-box.) Beyond the 'Up starting signal' and which is seen in the 'on' position—No. 2, is the sand drag and which was inclined at 1 in 8. The points here were some 600 yards from the signal box and were considered too far for mechanical operation—hence the hand generator. No. 28—the 'down home' is in the 'off' position although it is likely this was purely for the benefit of the photographer. Again standard GWR track fittings have been used, whilst not visible is that with the exception of the track in advance of the 'Limit of Shunt' indicator, track circuiting was provided in the vicinity. B/Box 397/8.

GWR Official View.

after passing his box. Meanwhile the box shook gently. A steady stream of wagons gently vibrating the floor, frame and shelf, and with the occasional vehicle perhaps wining more than its neighbours as it passed.

One of Bill's duties was to observe each train as it passed, ensuring there were no obvious defects, hot-axle boxes or the like. There were none, although Bill remained vigilant until the last vehicle, the guards van came in sight and already moving a lot faster than the

first vehicles, an indication that the engine was again pulling hard but still able to accelerate its heavy train. The guard waved at Bill as he passed, both in greeting and an acknowledgement that all was in order. Bill himself responded and having glanced to see the tail lamps were correctly lit walked again to the Whitchurch machine pressed twice on the plunger to indicate 'on-line' to Ken Alexander at Whitchurch. Without waiting for a reply he returned to the train register entering the time of his 'on-line' as 6.48 a.m..

He now had to collect the token deposited by the crew and as he headed for the stairs the opportunity was taken to replace No. 28 restoring it to danger. The plunger would not be required for this, the safety feature being that a signal could always be restored to danger at any time although for normal working this would not be done until the train was both clear of the signal together with any points or turnouts locked by the lever being in the reverse position. In the still air of the morning the trains' progress could be heard, it would soon reach the summit of the line after which the crew would have an easy time as it was then downhill almost all the way to Whitchurch.

Reaching the 'set-down' horn or catcher, Bill stood on the small wooden step to reach the carrier casually hanging from the hook. Retrieving the item he returned again to the 'box, separating the token from the carrier and hanging the latter again on one of the hooks. Before restoring the Woodhay token to the machine he quickly checked its wording, and then placing it in the slot turned the piece into the machine and allowed it drop into one of the slots. Gathering the duster again and which he had placed ready on top of the token instrument, he tapped out 'Train out of Section' to Woodhay and then still with duster in hand restored signals 27 and 26 to 'on' by returning their levers to 'normal' in the frame. An answering '2'-1' came from the gong.

Bill's next actions were as per his telephone call of a few moments earlier. '2 – pause – 3' to Woodhay asking the road for the light engine and which Bert at the latter place acknowledged immediately. Bill could now obtain the token for the light engine and he did so although leaving it hanging in the slot at the top of the instrument for now.

Before the engine could proceed though, he first had to reverse the crossover at the north end, and this he would do using the motor points No. 22. The actual crossover was several hundred yards from the signal points and so when the loop had been extended in 1942/3 and the new signal box provided, a hand generator was installed to operate the turnout. As a reminder to the signalman that No.22 was electrically operated the lever – painted black at its lower half and blue above, was some 4" inches shorter, its movement simply re-arranging the locking under the frame and not connected to a long length of point rodding.

The operation of No. 22 was also unique in the frame in that first Bert pressed the release plunger above and pulled the lever part way to a notch almost 1/3rd *(officially referred to as position 'B')* of the way across.

The plunger movement did not also require him to hold this down whilst he first moved the lever and so on pressing the centre he first heard the click from downstairs and indicating that the lock had ' picked'. It would remain this way for several seconds allowing the signalman time to move the lever at will. He now moved to the hand generator, or 'hurdy-gurdy' and which consisted a large metal box on an angle iron type frame protruding from which was a steel handle reminiscent perhaps of the starting handle on a lot of motor cars of the period. Affixed to a backplate attached to the machine was the indicator referred to and which for the moment stated 'normal' and meaning the crossover was set in the straight ahead position. Operation of the machine was also similar to that of a car-starting handle in that it was necessary to turn the handle until the generator had produced enough electricity to move the points. The indication that this had occurred being given by the indictor changing to 'Points Reversed'. Lever 22 could then be pulled over to its new position fully reversed so completing the locking within the frame. Whilst completing this task Bill would no doubt hope that after several hours of lack of movement the cold atmosphere would allow the electrical circuitry to work and no doubt with not a little trepidation Bill first pulled the lever mid way in the frame before commencing to turn the hand-generator at the same time as carefully watching the indicator above.

As he was on his own Bill would have been relieved the equipment had not chosen this occasion to malfunction. Generally it was very reliable but when failures did occur the options were either to remove the handle from the machine and walk out to the crossover using the handle like a key to turn the motor on the ground by hand, or send the train 'wrong-road' through the station This latter action could involve much extra work on the ground if it was a passenger service, as point clips would be needed for any movement over what were then facing points that were not equipped with a lock. Sometimes a member of the station staff or one of the gang could be cajoled to assist in this task but it was noticeable that whenever it was necessary there was usually never anyone around. *(Points both mechanical and power were also temperamental in extremes of temperature. When it was very cold a thin film of ice and rust builds up on the 'slide-chairs' and between the 'switch-blade' and the 'stock-rails', this has the effect of making the first movement 'stick a bit'. If they have been properly greased it does not happen as grease freezes at a much lower temperature, unless it has been washed away by rain!)*

He could now record the time of the 'Is Line Clear?' to Woodhay of a few minutes or so earlier, and which was recorded as 6.50. a.m.. The next task would be to pull lever No. 2, the up starting signal and this Bill did again releasing the electrical lock first with its plunger. As with No. 28, signal 2 was invisible to Bill from his position and so he would verify its movement by observing the electrical repeater.

His final act would be to collect the token from the machine place it in a carrier and give it to the engine crew. Some drivers would send their fireman to the signalbox as soon as they sensed they could go but this crew remained resolutely on their footplate and so Bill again ventured outside reaching up to the fireman from ground level. 'Right away Woodhay' he called to them although the crew seemed in no particular hurry to get away and it was all of four minutes before the engine was on the move northwards. Possibly then this was overtime for them!

Bill could track their progress initially from the signal box as Track Circuits '1T' and which extended from the tips of 20 points along the platform to the north end of the loop, '22T' and then '28T' recorded their progress. He also sent the requisite '2 beats' as 'on line' to Woodhay, recording this as taking place at 6.54 a.m.. With the track circuits in their black plastic cases showing the light engine was well on its way north, Bill could restore No. 2 and re-set the road for a movement to arrive in either direction. Indeed the provision of catch point.s and sand drags at either end of the loop had assisted greatly as two trains were now allowed to arrive simultaneously, this facility another part of the war time improvements of 15 years earlier.

All that was left now was to await 'Train out of Section' from both Whitchurch and Woodhay that each had arrived safely. This would not be likely for perhaps 10 minutes as the Washwood Heath had only been on line for perhaps six minutes and it would take around 15 to clear the section. Likewise the light engine would take about 10 minutes to clear Woodhay so for the moment there was time then for that cup of tea, perhaps a glance at yesterday's newspaper and maybe even a necessary trip to the singularly uninviting asbestos 'privy' outside. Bill would invariably take his lamp on these occasions, the limited shelter afforded sometimes even sort after by foxes and the like, it's hard to tell under these circumstances who would be the more startled Bill or the fox! Bill would be well used also to the solitude associated with his work, most signalmen preferred it that way. Often a lifetime spent in ones own company at work would make time outside of working hours all the more pleasurable.

Any opportunity though for an uninterrupted 10 minutes

of peace that morning though, were shattered by the sound of feet slowly crunching on the ballast nearby and followed by the door to the box being opened. Then came the sound of boots echoing noisily on the stairs and the sight of one of the permanent way gang, maybe Bennie or Fred addressing him from the stairs. The p/way men would rarely venture all the way into the box, respectful of the state of the floor and mindful also of likely effect hob-nail boots would have. The purpose of the visit though was more than social and so after a brief exchange of pleasantries Bill would be advised as to where the gang were likely to be working that day and if and when an occupation would be required. On this occasion Bill was advised that the gang would indeed want the occupation key to go towards Highclere - and meaning occupation of the line was required, in the gap between trains sometime after the 9.26 from Newbury. At this point there would normally be almost a two-hour gap in the services, but a lot also depended on the running of the 7.52 goods from Newbury and if any wagons were required to be put-off at Burghclere. Bert would normally be told of this in advance in the form of a 'box-to-box' message but as the train was probably still shunting at Newbury he would have no means of finding out as yet. The gang would have to check again nearer the time. As Bill returned to his chair the omnibus phone rang out the code, '4 pause 1' on its high pitched but flat sounding bell. This was someone calling on the circuit to Burghclere, each box on this circuit having its own code which they alone would respond to. Lifting the handset Bill listened for an instant to make sure no one else was talking and then answered, 'Burghclere'. This time it was another member of the gang telling him they would probably also want the key to go south sometime in the same gap. Bill's reply was again the same, although possibly also a bit gruff this time as he had now been interrupted twice and besides his tea was probably getting cold!

With the clock now showing 7.05 a.m., the Whitchurch bell again rang out '2 pause 1' although except to all but the trained ear the sound was that of three continuous notes. This was 'Train out of Section' from Ken Alexander, Bill acknowledged it and dutifully recording the time in the register. The next move from Ken would be the first 'up' passenger service due to leave Sutton Scotney at 7.33 a.m.. Bill could anticipate being asked for this train from Whitchurch around this time although much would still depend on how the down goods was progressing and whether, unknown to him for the moment, the passenger may have been delayed somewhere further south. For the present though that was again in the future and as he pondered this thought the Woodhay gong banged into action with the 'out of section' code for the light engine.

Around this time also the early turn station staff would be arriving for duty, usually Bessie Sheerman, sister of the p/way man referred to earlier and who would cycle down to the station from the cottage they shared alongside the main A34 road about one mile from the railway. Bessie's first tasks would be to open up the booking office and prepare any parcels that had been left the night before ready for the passenger service. This would be just after 8.0 o'clock and she always seemed to find plenty to do to occupy her and was a rare visitor to the signal box.

For the moment then Bill may have decided it was breakfast time and keeping a few chickens in a small run adjacent to the station house meant it would often be boiled eggs for breakfast. Again the GWR had years ago considered the welfare of their staff, for the clockwork timer intended for the motor points could be activated at the point the eggs had commenced to boil and would whirr away for exactly three minutes culminating in a more rapid wining sound and clunk to impart the requisite time had passed. Of course it real use was when restoring the motor points within the first three minutes of setting, the system dictating that the lever could not be moved until the requisite time had elapsed and so allowing for a possible train movement. Yet another example then of 'fail-safe' although in practice if is unlikely the engineers at Reading could had realised the timer within its neat glass case would be used more for the needs of the inner man. As an egg cup Bill could also well have used a lever collar. The standard circular GWR lever collar of ideal size to both hold an egg and catch any spillages. Far better designed then than other types of reminder collar used by other railway companies.

With a clear view now in the morning light Bill could look towards the station where Bessie would probably be bustling around in and out of the various offices and rooms. Bill himself occupied the former stationmasters accommodation at the station and had done so since 1938 he would also remain at the station long after closure achieving the dubious distinction of being the last signalman on duty in August 1964.

But that was to be in years to come and returning then to

22 January 1958 at 7.39 a.m. there was a single beat on the bell from Whitchurch. Again Bill roused himself answering both this and the subsequent '3 pause 1' request for the first up passenger service. This was the 6.28 a.m. departure emanating from Totton near Southampton and which called at all stations to Newbury and then Reading. The train was put 'on-line' ten minutes later but Bill could not of course 'ask on' to Woodhay as the 7.45 a.m. from Newbury would be due to arrive from the opposite direction around the same time. This was confirmed as three minutes later at 7.48. a.m. with one beat on the gong followed by three-pause-one. At the same time two further beats received from Whitchurch to indicate the train was on its way towards him. Seven minutes later at 7.55 a.m. and two further beats were received indicating that the down train was on its way from Woodhay although it would be a little while before it arrived as it would call at Highclere mid section. Likewise the up service would be making its own intermediate stop at Litchfield.

With the road now set for the both the first 'up' and 'down' movements Bill could return to await developments. Officially the up passenger train was three minutes down and so may have been slightly checked by the goods further south. In reality that would cause few problems at this stage as it was booked three minutes waiting time at Burghclere anyway. It looked then, as the remainder of the day should be straightforward.

To the untrained eye it would appear as if the signalman at a location such as Burghclere would do nothing for perhaps an hour between trains, but this was hardly true as long after the last movement had left the station Bill would be awaiting the code from the next signal box to indicate the train had arrived safely and complete - 'out of section' whilst he would likewise have to respond to an approaching train some time before it actually appeared.

Glancing towards the station Bill may have noticed a few intending passengers waiting for their respective services. A census carried out during 1958 revealing that the 'up' train would gain four additional passengers here although only 'one' would join the down train.

Opposite page; - Porter 'Clarry' Potter observes the arrival of BR 'Class 4' No. 76016 at Burghclere in 1958. As is referred to in the text, the lack of passengers in both this and other views of passenger trains is all too apparent. (The head-code is noted; clearly incorrect for the service and which should be a single disc—or lamp beneath the chimney.) Besides his portering duties and which he shared with Bessie, 'Clarry' was also responsible for the signal lamps at Burghclere, Highclere and Litchfield. These all required attending weekly and he would likewise ensure that those illuminating the ground signals and token pick-up / set-down posts were dealt with.

Courtesy; Mike Esau.

Within the locking there would be nothing now preventing Bill from pulling off the requisite signal – No. 1, to allow the up service to run straight in. In practice however, he would no doubt comply with Rule 39a and so wait until the driver could see the signal as an additional warning to the driver that the route was not set for through running. Likewise after receiving 'Train Entering Section' from Woodhay at 7.55 a.m., Bill could clear signal No.28., the drivers of both services would be expecting to stop at Burghclere anyway and so having completed the booking he went first to the south end of the frame to clear No. 1 and then did the same at the very last lever at the other end No. 28, Bill needing of course to operate the requisite brass release plungers in both cases.

No more could now be accomplished until the first train arrived. No token to obtain for either train to proceed as the sections either side of the signal box were currently occupied. Instead he waited, possibly looking south to see any sign of steam from the exhaust as the up train started away from the stop at Litchfield. This time though he could detect nothing and so anticipating its arrival time he was soon out of the signal box waiting to collect the token. He did not have long to wait either as the train was already in sight having passed under the road bridge. Bill collecting the token from the fireman of a BR Standard Class '4' in the 76xxx series as he stood with his arm outstretched. He could also make out the sound of his telephone ringing inside the box, it would probably stop before he returned – it did!

As he turned to return to the 'box Bill subconsciously noted a horsebox bringing up the rear of the train. The tail lamp was properly attached to this vehicle and so Bill was able to restore the token to the machine and immediately send '2 pause 1' to Whitchurch. Having received Ken's acknowledgement he immediately sent an additional '3 pause 1' and on receiving the code back was able to obtain another token for the pending down train. *(Signalmen would also rotate the tokens in use to equalise wear and tear, hardly necessary perhaps on what was now a quiet cross country route but all part of the general work practice that they followed throughout their careers. Likewise the token instrument had a small reminder key, which could be turned to 'Token out for up - or - down train' and again a visual reminder of whether a train was coming or going away from the signal box. Despite not being any part of the electrical circuitry most men would use this out of habit and indeed visiting Inspectors would expect it.)*

The record for the entry shows the codes to have been sent and received at 8.01 a.m., the train by now simmering quietly in the platform and with track circuit

No. '1T' which ran through much of the 'up' platform now showing occupied. Years earlier this would have been a Winchester turn although consequent upon the closure of the shed at Bar End, Eastleigh had taken over the former 'Chesil loco and crew duties using their own Eastleigh based locomotives.

Bill could restore signal No. 1 to danger and immediately alter the position of the south end crossover by restoring No. 6 to normal and immediately pulling 16 and 15 to the reverse positions.

Signals 28, 27 and 26 could also now be pulled - in that order after which he now had a choice as to whether to use the equipment to effect a token change as the pending 'down' service departed or effect a hand exchange. Probably the former would be the case and so after completing the entries in the book Bill would venture outside to place the token in the carrier.

The last few minutes had seen what was in effect a flurry of activity and it was not over yet, for no sooner had he returned to the signal box than track circuit '28AT' moved to its occupied position followed by '22T' - the down train was almost at the station. It was just coming up to five past eight o'clock.

Bill stood up and looked through the end windows towards the station. His eyes took in the up train waiting quietly at the platform and the single passenger waiting on the down platform. Bessie was there too having crossed the line by the board crossing to meet the 'down' service and collect any tickets from arriving passengers. There would be none on this occasion.

Still without the train in sight, track circuit '28AT' returned to the clear position. Bill could now restore signal 28 to normal, which he did. Shortly afterwards No. '22T' also bounced back to its horizontal 'clear' position and which was the prompt for Bill to 'plunge' and then move the lever controlling the motor points part way back towards the 'B' position - normal - and where there was a notch in the frame to hold it in this position, and then wind the generator until the indicator showed 'reverse'. Possibly the thought would have crossed his mind again about the inconvenience of a failure occurring at this moment, but at Burghclere problems were few, unlike Whitchurch where it was common practice for 'wrong road' or even hand operation to be called for.

At this point both trains were now also basically on time. The public book showing the 'down' due to depart at 8.03 am and the up service at 8.04. They would each be a couple of minutes down but with the leisurely schedules allowed the crew would have little difficulty in making this up in either direction.

Bill again now had a choice. If the Guard of the 'down' service were co-operative he would give Bill a wave from the platform to indicate the train had arrived complete. Some men though would either forget or ignored this vital safety requirement and under those circumstances Bill could do nothing until he himself had seen the presence of the tail lamp on the last vehicle as it subsequently passed the box. Even so there was still the important matter of the token for the section which was in the possession of the engine crew and this would have to be restored first.

What happened at Burghclere on that occasion is not known, and was really of little consequence, for almost sensing they were slightly late, the 7.52 a.m. from Newbury bound for Whitchurch set off again hardly a minute after it had arrived. The Didcot 22xx making a sharp staccato bark as it blasted its way south, the crew changing tokens at the 'set-down / pick-up' posts outside the signal box. Bill watched then for the guard to acknowledge him and that the tail lamp was indeed present before sending the 2-beats to Whitchurch. The times were recorded in the register (8.05 arrived and 8.06 am 'on-line') and he could now venture outside to collect the token which had just been deposited.

He also had to ensure the token was replaced back in the instrument before sending 'out of section' to Woodhay. This was quickly done – and acknowledged and after which he dialled Woodhay and obtained his co-operation for the 'up' train to use the auxiliary token instrument in a few moments time. For the moment though he simply recorded 'out of section' to Bert as having taken place at 8.08 a.m..

There was nothing now preventing Bill from preparing for the 'up' train to depart but for a reason that is not known, the 'Call Attention' and 'Is Line Clear' codes were not recorded as being sent for a further two minutes until 8.10 a.m.. Indeed it may well have been that at this point the telephone rang again, this time the Yard foreman at Newbury to advise Bert the down local goods, and which according to the book was due with him at 8.54 a.m. had one wagon destined for his station. Bert was also told there was nothing for Highclere that day so it would probably be with him in plenty of time having also already left Newbury. A complication though that Bert would have to consider was that he was also advised the goods would need to stop mid-section after it had left him and collect a vehicle from Litchfield.

Now Bill's had to 'get theroad' for the 'up' passenger train and having cleared signal No. 2, Bill now went to the bank of telephones on the back wall and lifted the handset to dial Woodhay. He could have used the 'omnibus' circuit but there was the risk someone else might be chatting and so it was easier to use the private connection. It rung only once before Bert picked it up, "......6.32 ready to depart.....at the auxiliary in a minute, so I'll ask the road and then call again for the release.....". "...Right'o...", relied Bert, the handset crashing down on the rest again as Bert replaced the receiver.

The crew of the 76xx on seeing the signal move to clear, whistled briefly and within a moment had set off. This was Bill's time to call Woodhay again and letting the phone ring a couple of times he replaced the receiver before venturing straight away to the token instrument. He now held down on the ringing key anticipating that Bert would be doing the same and without waiting for the fireman to call from the hut. Almost immediately he noticed the needle flick satisfactorily and meaning the token had been obtained by the fireman who would have been watching for the two galvo' needles on the auxiliary instrument to both move away from their vertical position. Having obtained a token the fireman would now place this in a carrier, several hanging on hooks within the little wooden hut. The crew of the 76xxx that morning were also on the ball as almost immediately track circuit '22T' showed occupied followed by '28AT' and which was quickly followed by '1T' returning to clear. Bill could now send two beats to Woodhay and enter the times with a one-minute gap recorded in between. Again he annotated an 'X' in the remarks columns of both pages and followed by the letters 'AT' for auxiliary token use. There was little danger of the crew going without the token either, to do so was a potentially sackable offence, certainly one where automatic suspension would follow.

With the up passenger now well on its way to Highclere and all track circuits returned to 'Track Clear', he could now return No. 2 to 'on' and set the road again ready for the next movement. Once more then the crossovers at either end were altered to allow for a train to run in from either direction as the 7.52 a.m. goods would cross with 7.32 a.m. 'up' passenger from Southampton.

For the moment though all that was left was to ring Bessie in the Booking Office to advise her that one wagon was due. Bessie may well know what this was, a customer could already have been enquiring. Replacing the receiver he could now renew his acquaintance with his armchair - nearly every signal box had one and often of dubious origin! There would be time also for another

A wet day finds Didcot based 2251 class 0-6-0 No. 3210 waiting at Burghclere in charge of the 9.26 a.m. departure 9.07 a.m. from Newbury.) Situated in the 'six-foot' is ground signal No. 13 and which afforded access back into the yard from the 'up' platform. Track circuit '1T' also commences at the end of the platform and continued through to the starting signal invisible under the road-bridge.

Courtesy; E.T. Gill. (G 60)

glimpse at the newspaper - maybe a different paper passed to him by the guard of one of the trains. So far also he had been on duty just over three hours, there were still some 5 fi to go.

It was just 10 minutes before the bells and gongs demanded his attention again, for at. 8.20 a.m. Whitchurch confirmed the passenger had arrived and the section was clear and then just one minute later the gong from Woodhay informing the same for the line northwards. This was immediately followed by Bert at Woodhay asking the road for the 7.52 as a '2-2-3' and which was accepted by Bill although it would still be some minutes before the train was 'on line' to him.

The fact that he had been asked for the road meant the train was 'about Woodhay' - at least on the way from Enborne Junction and so he was expecting the two beats to indicate 'entering section' any moment. As it was the summons from Whitchurch came first. A single beat, and which when acknowledged by Bill was followed by '3 pause 1' as the request for the 7.32 a.m. passenger service from Southampton. This had occurred at 8.33 a.m. Meanwhile the goods was finally put 'on-line' to Bill at 8.36 a.m., some 15 minutes after he had first been alerted to its presence. Possibly the delay in the goods was due to the service shunting the yard at Woodhay. According to the working timetable the goods was already some minutes late but with no need for the train to call at Highclere that morning it should still be right time with him. Possibly then the crew had been kept busy in Woodhay yard - or more likely they were not in any hurry that morning!

At many stations there would be a direct telephone link between the signal box and the booking office, but at Burghclere this did not exist and so Bill had no means of advising Bessie the goods was 'on-line'. There was a Post Office telephone in the Booking Office and which the public could also use if required but this would mean contacting Control first who would then have to go through the exchange to get through to the station. Hardly necessary for what was a routine matter.

Bill's only concern now was the running of the goods and the fact that it should arrive in time for the section to clear and so not delay the 7.32 a.m. passenger on its trip north. This was certainly a risk if the crew of the goods were inclined that way. Of course it may have been that they had a 'dud' engine that day and so at this stage it may well have been that Bill would again take the opportunity to call his colleague at Woodhay to ascertain the likelihood of any potential problem. Whilst he was speaking on the phone the Whitchurch bell rang again – two beats this time, the passenger was on its way. It would though have to call at Litchfield en-route but even so should arrive in something like 12-15 minutes. For the moment though he made a mental note of the time until his conversation was ended. Walking then to the south end of the frame he plunged and pulled lever No. 1 and entered the time – 8.45 a.m. in the book.

Goods services were invariably slower between stations anyway due to the lack of brake power available to the crew and so a running time of 15 minutes was to be expected from Burghclere. Anything more than this and there was the start of problems, although this was not the case and exactly to the anticipated time the track circuits clicked to 'occupied' followed almost immediately by the sound of an engine whistling. This was Bill's cue to pull No. 28 whilst a few seconds later the smokebox of Didcot based 22xx could be seen under the road bridge before coming juddering halt in the platform.

Bill observed the Guard, Fred Crockett, step out onto the platform and wave towards him. This was the sign the train was complete and at which point Bill could also take the opportunity to restore signal No. 28 to 'on' by returning the lever to 'normal' in the frame. Next came the 'hurdy-gurdy' again to change the motor points allied to No. 22 and its requisite release plunger. *(For this he would first restore the lever about 1/3rd in the frame - position 'D' and then turn the 'hand-generator. When the indicator showed 'N' he could push the lever fully back to its normal position ignoring position 'B'.)* Bill noticed also that the Guard using his shunter's pole between the buffers of two of the wagons part way along the platform. After which he climbed aboard the footplate as the engine slowly set off towards Bill with its reduced load, most of the train remaining in the platform.

Unseen by Bill the Guard of the goods would have ensured the handbrake in his van was screwed down hard before leaving the various wagons in the platform. *(One afternoon years before, a horsebox had been uncoupled from a down train next to the box and prior to being hand shunted back towards the goods shed. The signalman on duty was assisting and applied the hand brake. But unknown to him this was faulty and the moment the couplings were released it slowly ran back towards Highclere complete with horse and groom inside - subsequently 'see-sawing' back and forth on the switchback gradient to Highclere until finally coming to rest in the dip between the stations. The 'box was eventually rescued by the engine of the next 'up' train to arrive at the station, whilst shortly afterwards a catch point was provided in the down main. Bill had not been on duty that day but he knew who was, there had of course been an enquiry although no one was disciplined.)* After that everyone had taken more care although since 1943 and the provision of the sand drags and spring points a re-occurrence then was less likely, but he did not want it to happen on his shift.

The presence of the goods train also spoiled Bill's view of the up platform and any passengers who might be waiting for the coming passenger train. There were just two and making then a total of just five who would be in the train as a whole. (Later one would join at Highclere - but one of the original five would also leave, whilst three would join at Woodhay. This would make then a grand total of eight to depart at Newbury. Statistically it was then the quietest train on the line in either direction and clearly running at a loss.)

The engine of the goods together with two wagons behind the tender pulled slowly forward coming to rest just to the rear of the starting signal – No. 27. As it did so Bill started to make his way out of the box towards it. He actually got there first and had to wait a few seconds before reaching up to grasp the token from the fireman. As he did so he called up to the crew, "……the 7.32 is off Whitchurch, should be here anytime, wait for the signal…….", and turning on his heel he returned to the box.

Bill could now return the Woodhay token and ask the road for the passenger which would shortly be with him. Both actions were recorded as taking place at 8.51 a.m. after which Bill could immediately get ready to place the token in the carrier ready to be exchanged by the crew of

No excuses for repeating the use of this particular view from other publications, but it is still one of the very few to depict a pick-up goods on the DNS and also at Burghclere-unfortunately for the text perhaps in the wrong direction! The engine is of course No. 2240, a regular performer on the line in the BR era and perhaps unusually with a horse-box attached to a goods train. Presumably this one was empty as they would otherwise normally go by passenger train. Two ground signals are visible in this view, that facing the camera, No. 10 and which allowed traffic back across the running lines-it's use indeed referred to in this narrative. The other ground signal, and which can only be seen from the rear, was No. 18, and which function was to guard the exit of the yard back into the 'up' line.

Courtesy; Mike Esau.

the 'up' train. This action probably took him, say 2-3 minutes after which he would pull Nos. 1 and 2 to allow the train to both enter and leave the station. (The likelihood is that he would not pull the home signal – No. 1 allowing the train to enter until he had placed the token in the carrier. Bill would have been well aware the passenger was due any moment and if the crew did not see the token waiting for them would assume they were to use the auxiliary instrument. With a token already obtained from the signal box for them this could not be done and so it was common practice to 'check' a train outside for a brief moment if there was a chance it might

arrive before the signalman was really ready.)

As it was Bill had only just returned to the 'box before the whistle of an approaching engine alerted him. This was the 7.32 a.m., and which had made good time from Whitchurch, just eleven minutes inclusive of the Litchfield stop. The engine was a clean B.R. Standard Class 4 in the 76xxx series and with three coaches behind, two of which were still in chocolate and cream livery. As the third coach passed him Bill was able to observe the tail lamp in place and also notice the token in its carrier swinging gently from the catcher where it

Through freight traffic was slowly building on the DNS throughout the 1950's and continued almost until the very end. Gradually too BR 'Standard' designs became more commonplace on these workings and culminating in the '9F's on the heavy oil and petrol trains between the Midlands and Fawley. This time though it is a Class '4' 4-6-0 No. 75066 in charge of a mixed freight and which is passing the 'box southbound. Just ahead of the engine is the cover for the facing point lock—No; 15.

Courtesy; P.W. Goulder.

had been dropped by the fireman a few moments earlier. This was also another former Winchester turn although now Eastleigh men were in charge, the former Bar End Drivers and Firemen scattered between the sheds at Eastleigh, Didcot and Reading.

Bill's next job was to retrieve this token - the shunting would have to wait for a moment, but before leaving the signal box he replaced No. 1 to danger. In reality there was no need for him to have done this at that time. Nothing else was due from Whitchurch and indeed nothing could come arrive as the token was still out for the recently arrived train. Old habits though based on safety remained paramount, and Bill's actions would be to present a 'danger - stop' signal from the Whitchurch direction. As the noise of the lever returning died away

only then did he make his way down the stairs letting his hand run gently down the banister rail as he did so. The token from the passenger train was still swinging gently on the catcher at this time and Bill retrieved it easily noticing as he did the passenger already just leaving to head north. Returning to the box he separated the token from the carrier as before belling – or should it be gonging (?) two beats to Woodhay. He then walked to the south end of the box – token instruments were placed at opposite ends of the signal box in accordance with the section of line they controlled, returning the Whitchurch token, restoring the manual indicator to its vertical position, and sending '2 pause 1' to Ken. The time was 8.57 a.m. and the passenger service had waited just one minute at his station. The crew were certainly enthusiastic as well, perhaps it was pure 'joie di vivre' at having an engine that was steaming well for Bill had not noticed any wheezing or leaking steam anywhere as it had passed. With the train now well on its way to Highclere and all track circuits showing 'clear' he could also now restore No. 2 to 'on' and then start to deal with the shunting operation.

The first action now was to allow the shunt to draw forward and so it was necessary to restore bolt No. 6 to normal, pull the crossover No. 16 and bolt it by pulling No. 15. At this stage the down starting signal No. 27 was free but before pulling it Bill also reversed No. 6 again - it would be needed in a moment anyway. The down starting signal bounced slightly as it was pulled into the 'off' position almost immediately after which the 22xx began to move forward. As the engine and wagons slowly passed the 'box Bill could see the Guard standing in the 'six-foot' between the running lines ready to raise his hand to tell the driver to stop when he was clear of the yard points. Even though the engine was only travelling forward slowly its two wagons still jolted forward and back when it stopped, the next move now again down to Bill who's job it would be to reverse crossover No. 9.

In order to achieve this Bill had first to replace No. 27 and then he could pull No. 9. The trouble was the yard points were rarely used by this time, indeed goods tended to handled at the station perhaps just 2-3 each week and in consequence both the points and detection were not always easy to move. Covering the lever handle with the duster he first released the catch and then pulled hard. The movement was such that despite the points not being far outside the 'box they were still quite stiff - not helped no doubt by the cold and possible odd pockets of snow blown between the blades. With the lever now reversed he could pull No. 7 and then No. 8. Both of these were 'dummies' or to be more accurate ground signals, No. 7 allowing the train to reverse back 'wrong-road' along the 'down main' and No. 8 permitting entry to the yard itself. They were also pulled in that order - the direction the train was to proceed. By rights the engine and wagons should also have gone past No. 7 –

and which stood at the base of the up home signal although in practice the wagons had not even reached it – again normal practice, provided of course there wasn't an Inspector around! Lever No. 7 responded normally, but as he pulled No. 8 Bill could detect it was not right. The lever came over almost as if he was pulling against a tensioning spring and with it fully reversed in the frame he looked out to check the position of the ground signal, No. 8, and which still showed 'on' despite the position of the lever.

Releasing No. 8 again the lever flew back into the frame again, its very action indicating a wire stretch. Bill now had to restore the crossover No. 9 and 're-stroke' (pull it again) to attempt to ensure the slides on the detection outside moved across enough. Before he could do this however he had to restore No. 7 again and also make sure the engine was still stationary. It was. So lever No. 7 was returned to normal followed by No. 9.. then pull 9 again followed by 7 and then 8, this time the movement felt different as well and Bill could visually check by looking outside it had correctly responded. With a brief 'toot' on the whistle the engine began to move slowly back, the guard by now standing alongside a single box van the end of which protruded from the goods shed.

At no more than a slow walking pace the engine and wagons creaked and groaned their way across the crossover towards the goods shed. Fred Crockett was leaning on his shunters' pole next to what was an empty van, it had been delivered full a few days earlier and would now be collected. The engine stopped - again at the guard's direction and waited for him to couple up - a quick flick of the wrist with the pole resting on the buffer stocks and it would have been accomplished in an instant. At country stations shunting would usually be the responsibility of the guard although some men would attempt to get the local porter to do their work for them. Here at Burghclere, Bessie was more than a match for most of the men and they would not attempt to shirk from their normal responsibilities.

Opposite page—top: The view looking south from the 'down' platform and for the moment devoid of passengers and trains. Aside from the signal box and permanent way hut, the various buildings changed little in the 80 or so years the railway was open whilst the neatly cut bushes and gardens had been a feature for many years'

Courtesy; Lens of Sutton.

Opposite page—lower; The fireman of No. 7324 collecting the token as he passes the signal box, probably around 1957/8. Jack Green recounts one particular driver from Didcot who was regarded as quite mad. On goods services he seldom reduced speed through the loops as was required and would insist on catching the tokens himself as he did not trust his fireman at the speeds he would be travelling. To complete the picture he also always wore his cap back to front!.

Courtesy; P.W. Goulder.

Devoid of passengers, the scene from a Newbury bound train departing the station circa 1958. Despite the lack of passengers there was considerable traffic in the form of cakes and groceries received at the station throughout this period, and bound for the various stores at Etchinswell and Kingsclere—the latter would be collected by the customers delivery van. The cakes would arrive in sealed boxes until one day the customer started complaining the seal had been tampered with and items were missing. Bill and Jack suspected they knew the culprit—the lad porter at the time, and laid a trap to catch him. He was indeed caught—red handed, and in the lamp hut where he had taken to pass his break, supplementing his own food with cakes. He was summarily dismissed by the District Inspector.

Courtesy; Mike Esau.

As the engine came to rest Bill returned the two dummies, Nos; 7 and 8 to danger. This was now the danger time during the shunting process, for the lever controlling the crossover No. 9 was now free and could be moved in the frame despite the fact that the engine and wagons was standing on one end. Bill had been to signal boxes where the man on duty would use a reminder collar over the lever at this point and indeed he would probably do this himself in poor weather. Today though he had a clear view and so instead he pulled No. 10 – to allow the train to leave the goods shed and also No. 27 to allow it to pull forward onto the single line.

Again the engine came slowly forward, stopping once

more with the van now clear of the crossover. Bill restored No. 10 and 27, then No. 9 to normal. He then quickly checked through the north end window that the crossover was indeed fully over before reversing No. 7 and giving a wave to the guard who in turn started to wave the engine back onto the train.

The wave from Bill was an important part of the operation, as Bill was checking for himself the crossover had returned to normal on the ground as well. The move the engine and wagons now had to make was to place the van that had been collected from the goods-shed back onto the train and as such the vehicles would be running in a facing direction against No. 9 and for which there was no signal detection. The visual check then was just part of the normal operational safety procedure.

The train came back slowly the guard again conducting the engine. As it passed the 'box Bill could return No. 7 again to normal whilst the engine slowly buffered up against the waiting wagons. Again the guard coupled the train before then undoing the coupling between the van and wagon that was to be left. Bill in the meanwhile had again pulled off No. 27 to again allow the engine to pull forward once more.

This time the though the crew seemed in no hurry and the minutes ticked past slowly without any apparent move by the loco. Already the clock was showing 5 past 9 the departure time in the WTT for the goods towards Whitchurch and there was still the Burghclere wagon to place near the shed. Had the crew got a move on they could have been ready to leave by now and still have time to shunt at Litchfield without delaying the following passenger service. The problem now was the next down passenger service, due off Newbury at 9.07 a.m. and Woodhay at 9.15 .a.m.. If it was running to time he would not be able to accept the train as the goods was still occupying the down platform.

As if reading his thoughts however, the engine gave a brief 'toot' and again began to move forward, the Guard again walking alongside. Once more Bill waited until it had come to rest before restoring No. 27 and then reversing Nos; 9, 7 and then 8. The previous movement also seemed to have cleared the sluggishness of the crossover

Busy times at Burghclere in March 1960, and with Nos. 76011 and 31795 double heading a Bevois Park (Southampton) to Didcot oil train possibly due to the non availability of the booked '9F ' - or it may simply have been a means of avoiding light engine working. Waiting outside the box is No. 31794 on another freight, although this time empty vehicles. The crew of the 'up' service would have just given up the Whitchurch-Burgchlere token— configuration 'D' - yellow, and would have collected the 'Blue' configuration token for the section to Woodhay. (When the boxes either side of Burghclere—viz; Lithcfield and Highclere, were closed in 1955, the token colours and configurations were not altered at Burghclere. Instead it was Woodhay and Whitchurch where re-configuration took place.)

Courtesy; David Fereday-Glenn.

from last time for on this occasion 'the dummy' — No. 8 responded correctly and the train was soon backing in towards the shed again before leaving a single wagon of coal clear of the crossover and outside the shed. Watching the engine slowly backing Bill was alerted by the operation of the Woodhay gong as it tolled '2 pause 1', the previous passenger service had arrived at the latter location and the section was clear. The gong was not easily heard on occasions if there was a lot of outside noise and so the signalman would often look towards it and almost 'see' the sound as the hammer moved and the case vibrated slightly. All now depended on the running of the 9.07. a.m.. If the goods got a move on it could still depart ahead of the passenger, but as Bill walked to the Woodhay machine to acknowledge the code the engine was still stationary with little action seemingly taking place.

Unseen by Bill, the Guard would also have pinned down the brakes on the wagon before uncoupling, the actual coal in the wagon intended for one of the Newbury merchants and who with the wagon's arrival would use the station as a base for a few days whilst delivering in the local area. At some stage also the coalmen would physically push the wagon back along the siding to make unloading easier.

Once more Bill restored levers 8 and 7 and pulled Nos; 10 and 27. As he did so the Woodhay gong tolled out '3 pause 1' 'Is Line Clear?' for the 9.07 a.m.. Despite the fact that the actual section was clear, Bill did not have 440 yards clear ahead of the down home signal - his 'clearing-point' and as such he was not permitted to accept a train under Regulation 4. *(Regulation '5' applied where the section was clear only as far as the home signal could also only be used if it authorised in the Box instructions.)*

Instead he could only pick up the phone and speak to Bert at Woodhay to advise him of the situation. The response somewhat typical and direct and aimed by Bert at the engine crew was blunt, "………….what the ……are they hanging about at……..".

As Bill replaced the receiver, the engine came slowly forward again. Bill again changed the road by replacing Nos. 10, 27, 9 and then pulling No. 7. He then slid the window open and called to the Guard, "You're collecting one from Litchfield, right? – it was said almost as much as a statement as a question. "Collecting one", came the reply, and so confirming Bill's knowledge. Right that was it, the goods would have to pull forward and then set back into the up platform to clear the road for the down passenger, as to let it go would mean the section to Whitchurch would be occupied for quite some

time as they shunted at Litchfield yard, especially if they were as slow there as they had been with him. Bill had another quick confirmatory glance at crossover No. 9 to check it had restored and then continued, "…you are OK to set back onto your train, then pull forward clear of the loop and set back into the up…..the down passenger has been offered from Woodhay". The guard replied with a wave and disappeared on the far side of the wagons towards the engine.

The next Bill saw was the Guard riding on the footplate. He had clearly imparted the information to the driver as the Fireman gave Bill the thumbs up as they passed. The engine slowed and stopped again with the remaining single wagon against its train. Bill in the meanwhile had restored No. 7 and pulled off the starter, No. 27. He could then turn to watch the guard mount his van again alongside the platform and quickly release the handbrake. The Fireman was also looking back along the platform, for the moment the green flag was visible, the engine again tooted and was on the move towards the signal box. It passed him a few seconds later travelling at a fair rate for a goods train.

Of course at this stage the train could only proceed within station limits, and meaning as far as the advanced starting signal, but that was still some 200 yards clear of the south end turnout for the loop and the goods would easily fit into the space. (Had it not Bill would simply have sent 'Shunting into Forward Section' to Ken Alexander at Whitchurch.)

Another wave from the Guard confirmed the train was clear of the points and Bill could then restore No. 27 followed by the bolts at either end of the crossover – Nos; 15 and 6 and then No. 16 for the crossover. He then quickly pulled No. 6 again to bolt the crossover for the goods followed by the home signal, No. 1 to allow the train to reverse into the up platform.

With the road now set and the clearing point restored, his next job was to acknowledge the '3-1' from Woodhay and this he did at 9.14 a.m.. It had taken just three minutes for the engine and wagon to set back onto its train, couple-up and then pull forward clear. "Shows they can do it when they want to…..", mused Bill to himself, at the same time watching the goods slowly reversing with the Guard beckoning back to the driver from his van.

As it turned out it was not until 9.18 a.m. that Woodhay put the passenger train 'on-line', with Bill immediately 'offering-on' to Whitchurch and which was accepted. Bill pulled off No. 28 followed by 27 and then 26. Having withdrawn the token he placed this in a carrier and made his way outside to put it in the pick up position. Returning to the box after this it was again now a question of waiting, this situation not untypical of a crossing place on any single line either. Periods of quiet followed by an intensity of movement before settling down again. It was almost as if the whole station, signal box, and staff needed a rest between trains.

Unbeknown to Bill as well, matters were occurring elsewhere that would affect him shortly. The passenger service now running quietly into an almost deserted Highclere Station and departing shortly afterwards after collecting a solitary passenger. As it left Highclere it attracted the attention of the Ganger and who was the cause then of the 'phone ringing in Burghclere 'box. Bill uprooted himself from his chair again and set down his cup of tea on the desk. 'Burghclere', he answered. Back came a Hampshire voice, 'Morning Bill, Fred told you earlier,...........we wants the key after the down passenger arrives with you...............give us a call at the 'box will yeh....?' Right -ho", replied Bill and replaced the receiver. The message to Bill was clear enough, the Highclere Gang wanted a release of the occupation key as soon as the line was clear again. He would advise the gang at Highclere by calling them on the phone that remained inside the former Highclere Signal Box when the time was right. This though would also require the co-operation of Bert at Woodhay and so Bill's next task was to contact Bert by phone to inform his colleague. That done he could again sit down with his by now lukewarm cup of tea.

But not for long. The first telephone call had come as the passenger was leaving Highclere and the running time to Bill was about five minutes at the most, accordingly as Bill moved back towards his chair, Track Circuit No. 28AT clicked as the black bar moved from its horizontal to 45° position and closely followed by No. 22 in like manner. Bill looked back towards the station and could already see an engine appearing under the bridge and slowing for the platform. It came to rest almost alongside the waiting engine of the goods, no doubt an intentional act by the crew so they could exchange greetings - or more usually ribaldry with the other crew. With the track circuits clear, Bill restored No. 28 and entered into the book the time the train had arrived, 9.27 a.m.. By rights it should be on its way already, being 1 minute down at this stage, but again a minute or two was of minor consequence nowadays.

There were three passengers to join the train south that morning Bessie supervising matters from the platform and which also involved unloading two wicker boxes from the van. 'Pigeons', mused Bert, the engine now displaying a brief shot of steam from the whistle the sound of which reached Bill a fraction of a second later.

Approaching him the engine crew were looking out of the cab and accordingly Bill slid open the end window to hear any message as they passed, the fireman first depositing the token for the Woodhay section and then collecting the one placed by Bill. The engine slowed briefly as the driver shut off steam as they approached the box and no doubt to reduce the noise so Bill could hear, "...keep them buggers waiting back there, they held us up the other day.......", called a youthful voice, and which belonged to the fireman. He was grinning though, as was the driver.

Sliding the window closed Bill observed the tail lamp was in place, before he belled two beats to Ken. He recorded both the departure and 'on-line' times as 9.28 a.m., before venturing out to collect the token just deposited. Once back inside the signal box he could now return the token to the machine and then send 'out of section', remembering again to turn the reminder key to its normal position. The final act at this time was to restore levers 27 and 26 to danger and reset the road ready for the goods although this could not of course depart until the passenger train had safely reached Whitchurch.

He therefore restored numbers 15 and 16 in the frame to normal and which now meant that for the first time that day every lever was standing normal in the frame. With the south end crossover in its normal position meaning the road was set for the 'up' platform there was nothing else Bill needed to do and he could now again turn to the matter of the occupation key for the Highclere Ganger.

His first task then was to speak to Bert at Woodhay and ask him to hold down on the ringing key of the token instrument. This achieved he then dialled Highclere and which was answered almost immediately. After the customary ribald comments to Bill such as, "...thought you'd gone to sleep there, some of us have got work to do....", Bill replaced the receiver on the hook having also been told that the ganger would be coming through on his inspection trolley towards him. He then went to the slides on the occupation control instrument. Like the token instrument this was a large machine coloured red to the sides and front but with a flat wooden top instead of the semi-circular top of the token instrument. The occupation control instrument was fitted with a 'galvo' the same as the token instrument and accordingly Bill could observe that Bert was still holding down - the galvo being held over. Accordingly Bill could pull the left hand, control, slide out to its full extent after which he pressed the small brass button encasing the plate which stated 'Woodhay - Highclere'. This action energised a small electric coil within the Highclere occupation key instrument and allowed the word 'FREE' to appear in a small slot. The ganger could then remove the key and by so doing the 'galvo' dropped to vertical again. The action taken in removing the key had also locked the token system so that no single line token could now be obtained until the occupation key was restored. Finally Bill entered the time in the book.

Normally there would now be a break in the service of over an hour during which time Bill might well make it back to the Station House for lunch. He would of course have to advise his colleagues either side of his actions and such behaviour could not be undertaken if Harry Hillier, the Whitchurch Station Master was around. Harry's 'patch not only covered his home station but also Litchfield, Burghclere, Highclere and Woodhay although his colleagues either side would normally warn if '...'arry's about...''. *(Harry was a regular visitor on a Thursday afternoon and which was pay-day. He would always collect the money from the bank in Whitchurch in the morning - so there was at least very little likelihood of a surprise visit on a Thursday morning!)*

This morning though Bill was stuck waiting for the passenger to clear the section and which bell code was not received from Whitchurch until 9.43 a.m.. Immediately then Bill asked the road for the goods, sending it as a '3' and meaning 'Freight, Mineral or Ballast train stopping at intermediate stations.' Technically this was correct as the goods was due to collect the wagon from Litchfield in mid section to Whitchurch. Interestingly though Bill had received the train under the description '2-2-3' and meaning 'Ballast Train, freight train or inspection train requiring to stop in section'. It almost seemed to depend on who was working either side and how they themselves had no doubt received the code in the first place.

Ken at Whitchurch was well aware of the pending train and it was immediately accepted. Bill could then obtain a token and also pull off No. 26. The fireman attracted by the signal coming off and so meeting Bill at the foot of the box and saving him a walk.

It was though a further two minutes before the engine whistled up and started to move slowly forward, Bill watching for the tail lamp and finally sending 'on-line' to Ken at 9.45 a.m..

With the train now well on its way and past the starting signal, Bill restored No. 26 and pulled numbers 6 ready for next move, the 10.18 a.m. passenger from Eastleigh. For the moment however, he left the far end crossover

No. 22 as it was. The Highclere Ganger had occupation and as such could very well be about with his trolley. He would not take kindly to a turnout moving in front of him, as trolleys could not always be guaranteed to activate track circuits.

As it was Bill's decision was correct for just a few moments later came the sound of a small motor engine the sound of which then died. Again Bill was out of his chair and in time to see two men dismounting the small trolley. One now made his way to the permanent way hut whilst the other, and who Bill recognised as Bob Aldridge, the Highclere Ganger was making his way towards the 'box. Opening the door, Bob stamped his way upstairs and handed Bill the brass occupation key. Bob did not wait long, he was a man of the old school and like so many others worked on that basis, accordingly he came straight to the point, "...I'll be wanting to go on to Box 4 with the trolley shortly, alright to leave it where it is for now Bill...?" Bob Aldridge would have known the timetable and the times train times as well as Bill although he would have no knowledge of any specials that might also be running, hence the check with the signalman. Bill replied, "...fine, but I will need the section by 11.00 at the latest...". Bob nodded and set off towards the stairs again, he rarely stayed long chatting and like so many of the long service men maintained a basic and simple philosophy, "It's the Company's time.......", a throwback to the days of the old GWR, but long engrained in railwaymen regardless of their grade. The brass key that Bob would need to travel south with his trolley was for moment locked in the occupation key instrument within the signal box and would later require the co-operation of the Whitchurch signalman for its release. For the moment also it could not be obtained as a token was still out for the goods which was 'in section'. *(Like the tokens, each brass key had a different configuration and would only fit in one set of instruments. Unlike the token system however where there might perhaps be as many as 26 tokens for each section, although of course only one could ever be out at a time, there was only one brass occupation key per section. One of the responsibilities of the Ganger then being to always know in which instrument within the section the occupation key actually was.)*

Taking the occupation key just given back to him for the section from Highclere, Bill quickly turned it into the occupation key instrument and which was situated at the north end of the 'box. This was very much like a miniature token instrument and again with a semi-circular top, the type referred to by some signalmen as being like 'tombstones'.

Another regular performer on the DNS was No. 3206, seen here at the head of the 12.25 p.m. service from Newbury due at Burghclere at 12.43 p.m.

Courtesy; Great Western Trust

By rights now Bill should now have checked the operation of the token instruments by sending 16 beats to Woodhay as 'Testing instruments and Bells.' Nothing though is recorded in the book over this and the only entry instead refers to "Highclere OC Key 9/30. Res here 9/55". With Bob intending to travel south with the trolley again in the near future, Bill reset the road ready by restoring No. 6 and pulling 16 and 15.

Now at last he could relax for a while, although first he changed the loop points with the hand generator and No. 22 so the route was then set for the 10.18. a.m.. The final entry at this stage being at 10.05 a.m. when Ken belled to confirm the goods had arrived safely and the section was again clear. The goods had taken then 20 minutes between Burghclere and Whitchurch, a reasonable time when it was considered it was also required to shunt one

wagon mid way. Perhaps they had no-one to talk to at Litchfield!

This was also now the longest uninterrupted time in Bill's shift and which lasted until just before 10.50 a.m.. At this time Bill heard voices outside and the little petrol engine of the trolley coughed itself into action. The door also opened and another member of the gang arrived to ask for the occupation key for the section south towards Whitchurch. With the passenger train however due off Whitchurch at 11.07 a.m., Bill took care to remind him he only had a limited time as he would require the section again before this. Having been assured it would be restored correctly, Bill probably then advised Ken at Whitchurch of the situation, no doubt asking Ken to delay asking for line clear until 11.00 a.m. and at which point the passenger would be heading north mid section

Functional yet austere was perhaps the best way to describe the wartime 'boxes on the DNS and as with most signal boxes cold on occasions. Bill is seen here against the background of his workplace for so many years. It was also a trusting time of life for the box was never locked between shifts, only occasionally at weekends-and then the key was left under the doormat!

between Sutton Scotney and Whitchurch probably in the vicinity of the former loop at Lodge Bridge. With Ken holding down then on his token instrument - and with the key actually in the occupation instrument at Burghclere itself, Bill could then pull both of the slides on the control instrument and so release the brass key. This he handed to the man and then made the necessary register entry.

Again now came an interruption, this time the Eastleigh lineman intending to transfer some tokens from the signal box to the auxiliary instrument. This was a regular and necessary action, although usually Bill would have noticed Jim Eades, the Lineman getting off the train at the station. That morning however he may have been too busy to notice or perhaps he had walked through the section as the door opening downstairs had been the first clue there was to be a visitor. Bill recognised Jim and greeted him accordingly, Jim quickly telling Bill his intentions and then also 'phoning Bert at Woodhay to advise him also. Jim then used his key to open the top of the Woodhay instrument, this was only accomplished with some effort and by striking the knob on the top with his palm. "….must do something about that one of these days…….", he muttered. He never did, and the instrument top was destined to remain awkward for the remainder of its life. With the top now open Jim could lift the release lever by hand and by placing a token in the slot turn it out. He repeated the operation ten times before banging the lid down and locking it again. Checking the number of tokens again, he showed Bill who made an entry in the register. Jim then placed these in his shoulder bag and if Bill offered would probably

gratefully also have accepted a mug of tea. He may also have taken some carriers also, some signalman annotating the number of these that were to be moved to the auxiliary hut. *(The transfer of tokens to the auxiliary hut was required to replenish the stock there and so allow trains to use this facility when required by the service. The 1958 average was perhaps once or twice monthly. Tokens were also transferred between signal boxes either end of the same section to maintain a suitable number of tokens in the instruments at either end and when more trains ran in one direction than the other. Token transfers also always involved an even number of tokens, in such way the machines at either end of the section remained 'in-phase'.)*

Whilst this had been going on the little trolley had revved itself up and set off southwards. With the section south temporarily under 'Gangers Occupation', Bill had no need to pull any of the signals and his only action then would be to restore the crossover again ready for the pending passenger train once the trolley had disappeared from view. (Nos; 15, 16 and 6.)

True to his word also Bob Aldridge was on the 'phone again to Bill just five minutes later to state that the trolley was now clear of the line at Key Box No. 4. (To clear the trolley from the line, the men would have used some large poles - similar to scaffold poles and which enabled the little machine to be turned through 90° and lifted clear of the track. Once that was done, and not before, the brass key would be replaced in the instrument by the Ganger and Bill advised accordingly using the telephone situated for that purpose at each key box. *(Key Box No.*

4 was situated at 8m 14 chains from Enborne and just over 1fi miles then south of Burghclere Signal Box.)

Again Bill may well have tested the instruments to Ken although this is not recorded. Instead the next entry comes at 11.00 a.m. when Whitchurch asked Bill with '3 pause 1' for the 10.18 Eastleigh to Newbury. With the section restored and the crossover set, Bill accepted this straight away, receiving next the 'two beats for 'Train Entering Section' at 11.10 a.m.. So far that day Bill had also had little contact with Bessie at the Station, this was just the way things worked out although part of his task as Signalman would also be to try and advise her if a service was running unduly late – not easy with no telephone linking the signal box and booking office! With no crossing movement due Bill could also now 'ask on' to Woodhay straight away, and which was accepted immediately. The final stages being to use press each release plunger then pull off Nos. 1 and 2, enter the times in the book, and place the token for the section north in the pick up point opposite the signal box. The auxiliary instrument not needing to be used on this occasion.

The public book showed the train due to leave Burghclere at 11.22 a.m., but it did not in fact arrive with Bill until two minutes later at 11.24. a.m.. The engine a 'Southern' 'T9' coupled to three coaches this time in the then standard BR 'blood and custard' livery. The crew successfully exchanged tokens before pulling up at the platform to collect just three passengers who would join the six already in the train. No one alighted.

After a wait of just one minute the service was off again, Bill watching the train depart as he ventured back to his signal box with the token he had just collected from the set down point. He could now replace No. 1 to danger, restore the token to the instrument, sent '2 pause 1' to Whitchurch and also '2 beats' to Woodhay. Finally he would enter the times of the train leaving, out of section and entering section - all recorded at 11.25 a.m.. Finally with the train off his track circuits on its way north he restored No. 2 and reset the road with the relevant levers so as to admit a train from the Newbury direction and which would be the next scheduled move.

Under normal circumstances, the 10.18 a.m. would have crossed at Burghclere with the 9.50 a.m. through freight from Didcot to Eastleigh. Bill though had received a call from Southampton Control that this train was running late and accordingly it would be fitted into what was deemed a 'Q' path later on. These pathways were fitted into the timetable to accommodate both 'box to box' special workings and also out of course freight workings. The DNS at this time still receiving something like

3-4 'box to box' workings a week of this type. A 'Q' path then would accommodate an extra or out of course working without delaying the normal timetabled traffic.

With the train on its way north, Bill awaited the 'out of section' from Woodhay and which came at 11.35 a.m.. The next train would be 12.25 p.m. passenger from Newbury and in the meanwhile he could watch perhaps the antics of the coal merchant and his men as they struggled to push their loaded wagon back along the siding towards the open area and where it would make unloading a lot easier.

Perhaps then it was now time for a chat on the 'bus phone with one of his colleagues. Possibly to Arthur Watts temporarily relieving at Sutton Scotney that day as one of the regular men, Ernie Penny was away. Arthur was on the relief now and covered all of the remaining 'boxes on the DNS having formally been one of the regular men at Kings Worthy until that 'box was abolished along with Litchfield and Highclere in 1955.

He may also have spent some time on 'domestic' duties in the 'box. Traditionally Sunday mornings was the time spent cleaning and polishing but Burghclere was rarely open on Sundays, unless there was an engineers occupation and so both Bill and Jack would usually find some time during the week for such duties. Whatever Bill's actions for the next hour, nothing appertaining to the signalling is reported as he is next noted for acknowledging the 'Is Line Clear?' from Woodhay at 12.28 p.m. and ready for the train from Newbury. This was then put 'online' to him at 12.34 p.m.. and offered on by Bill to Whitchurch at the same time. After pulling off the signals, (Nos; 28. 27 and 26) he could venture outside with the token ready to place it ready for collection and after making the necessary entries, await the train.

This arrived at 12.43 p.m., an Eastleigh 'T9' again at the head of the three coach set, engine and coaches having originally set off from Didcot at 10.50 a.m. but then having laid over in the bay at Newbury for nearly 50 minutes. At this point the locomotive crew would also have changed, Eastleigh men taking over the service back towards their home territory and who had been at Newbury since their arrival on the 10.18 a.m. Eastleigh at 11.40 a.m..

This time there was no one to join the train, but Bessie did have two tickets to collect from passengers who alighted. The train set off almost immediately whilst Bessie and the others crossed the line behind it and by means of the board crossing at the north end of the platforms.

Once more Bill observed the tokens correctly exchanged before sending 'on line' to Ken at 12.44 p.m.. Venturing outside he collected the token, automatically then completing the next actions, of restoring this, sending the code north, returning the various signals to danger and completing the booking.

There remained now just one more crossing move before his shift would end – and one surprisingly where Bill appears to have omitted to record the customary 'X' in the remarks column of the book, possibly because it was an out of course working. This though could not take place until the section south to Whitchurch was clear. Bill had of course also restored the crossover at the south end so as to permit a train to enter from Whitchurch.

Accordingly at 12.46 p.m., Woodhay had asked the road for the delayed 9.50 a.m. through freight. It was put 'on line' to Bill at 12.50 p.m. the same time as Ken sent 'out of section' for the previous down passenger service.

Eight minutes later and Ken was sending '3 pause 1' for the 12.20 p.m. passenger from Winchester and which was put 'on line' to him just one minute later at 12.59 p.m.. Possibly then Ken had been busy as normally there would have been some few minutes between each code and the section had indeed been clear for several minutes. By rights the down freight would normally take perhaps 16 to 17 minutes to arrive with Bill, but today would be different and as the minutes passed there was still no sign of the train. Eventually the track circuit repeaters heralded its appearance some 20 minutes after leaving Woodhay and Bill could pull No. 26 to admit the train to the loop, the engine coming to rest just to the rear of No. 27 signal. Bill ventured down to collect the token from the fireman and who was audibly cursing the engine and the load. At the head the engine, a dirty looking 22xx was emitting great clouds of black smoke, a sure sign matters were not at their best on the footplate. Bill glanced back and received the customary wave from the Guard to confirm the train was complete. He could now return the token to the instrument and clear the section north before immediately asking on for the impending passenger service.

Back in the 'box the necessary levers were restored together with the activation of the 'hurdy-gurdy'. Then it was the tokens, Bill able to venture outside and place the token for the Woodhay section in the carrier just two minutes before the passenger train eventually arrived. This time it was a 43xx series 2-6-0 heading the train and with this time not just the customary three-coach rake but also with two horse boxes in tow. Perhaps then these had been the cause of the delay further south. The crew placed the token on the post as they passed ready for Bill to retrieve it.

He could now again reset the road for the goods and obtain permission for it to proceed. The engine crew though were not in any particular hurry and it was not until 1.16 p.m. that Bill was able to send 'Entering Section' southwards. The passenger service had in the meanwhile departed north, the Station providing just two additional passengers to join the compliment of 13 already in the coaches.

At least it was running to reasonable time as the section to Woodhay was cleared again at 1.25 p.m. but it was not until 1.40 p.m. that Ken could acknowledge likewise from Whitchurch. Twenty-four minutes running time then for the freight over a fraction more than six miles, small wonder is was late and getting later all the time.

The final part of Bill's shift would be to set the road again ready for the next move even though he would not be overseeing it. This would be the 2.0. p.m. passenger departure from Newbury – the 12.42 from Didcot and sometimes with 'City of Truro' at its head. Bill had occasionally stayed on to watch it pass but the engine was a common sight now but still on most days there would be a photographer or admirer to record its passage. Sadly despite recording the scene these individuals rarely travelled on the line, the 12.42 p.m. hardly better patronised by the fare paying passenger than any of the other services.

Bill's relief arrived at 1.45 p.m. in the form of Jack Green. Jack was the other regular man at Burghclere and occupied the nearest of the former lime workers cottages. After a few words as to the state of traffic that morning Bill signed the book recording officially 'W. Hiscock Off Duty 1.45 p.m..' The end then of another shift, there would still be hundreds more to come - the very next the following morning on early turn, Bill and Jack alternating weeks at early and late shifts. So it would continue also until August 9 1964 when Bill would receive 'out of section' for the very last time. He would though continue to live at Burghclere occupying the Station House for some years after the railway eventually closed and was lifted. The final years of his residence seeing the signal box stripped and vandalised, the very items he had worked with for so many years destroyed as belonging to a method of working no longer needed. In its final form then Burghclere Signal Box had a life of just 21 years, although the seeds of its demise could be witnessed by Bill and his colleagues all that time before, the lack of passengers meaning the end was for all to see a foregone conclusion.

June 1953, and the first day Southern region 'T9' class locomotives began working services north of Newbury. This is the view Bill would have had of a train entering the station —al'be'it slightly further distant. Bill would also have probably allowed the train to enter the station even if was at he time unable to proceed as the driver would know he was going to stop, it was only the through goods services that were 'cautioned'.

Courtesy; T. B. Sands.

DOWN TRAINS   **BRITISH RAILWAYS**

.... Signalbox .... day .... day of .... 19 ....

DESCRIPTION OF TRAIN	REAR SECTION					Train Arrived		Train Departed		ADVANCE SECTION					REMARKS
	Time described	Is Line Clear Received	Is Line Clear Accepted	Train entering Section Received	Train out of Section Sent	Line on	Actual Time	Line on	Actual Time	Time described	Is Line Clear Sent	Is Line Clear Accepted	Train entering Section Sent	Train out of Section Received	
										//					
		Wednesday													
		Bill Hiscock on duty 5/0 a													
1.50 W.O1	3/1	628	628	635	650						642	642	648	7.5	X
7/40 New	3/1	748	748	753	758	7.5	7.6				81	81	86	8.20	X
7/52 New	3/1	821	821	836	851	857		Canc 9/16							X X 10.51 / 0.11
9/7 New	3/1	911	914	918	930	927		928			918	918	928	943	X
		Highclere o cky 9/20 Res here 9.55.													
7/57 New	3	_above_						9.45			943	943	946	10.5	
12/25 New	3/1	1228	1228	1234	1246	1243		1244			1234	1234	1244	12.5	
9/50 Prin	1/4	1246	046	1250	1.11	1.11		116			1.14	1.14	1.16	1.40	
		Bill Hiscock off duty 1/45 Pm													
B. 3.01 Cable		7.5	10.21		.19	.20					7.10	.19	.30	.35	
	3/3	_from Woodhay 3.18 Q R 3p/5_													
B. 11/52 (Sat)		4.11	13	5.22		5.0		5.11			14.56	5.1	5.4		
P. 10/45 W.14.1		5.54	610	6.17		.47		.30			6.00	.30	.45		X
B. 7/12 TB		4.13	7.33	7.44		.47		.43			7.33	.43	.54		
F. 8/15 TB		8.51	5.17	9.10							8.51	9.17	9.32		
		H & Green off duty 10.40 Pm													

This and opposite page;

The actual register entries for 22 January 1958 and on which the text is based. Included is the complete day's service and so showing entries by both Bill Hiscock and Jack green.

TRAIN REGISTER BOOK

UP TRAINS

BR 24665/2

.... Signalbox.................. day........................ day of............................. 19.......

DESCRIPTION OF TRAIN	REAR SECTION					Train Arrived		Train Departed		ADVANCE SECTION					REMARKS
	Time des-cribed	Is Line Clear Received	Is Line Clear Accepted	Train entering Section Received	Train out of Section Sent	Line on	Actual Time	Line on	Actual Time	Time des-cribed	Is Line Clear Sent	Is Line Clear Accepted	Train entering Section Sent	Train out of Section Received	
						Jan 22	No 58								
Eng	7/3	621	627	630	642	642		654	650	650	650	647	7.5	X	
6/15 Bulk	3/1	739	739	748	8.1	8.1		9.11	810	810	811	821		X AT.	
7/32 Soton	3/1	833	833	845	857	856		857	851	851	857	98	X	
				at 10.5		Relined	Box No 4 + 50				10/55				
			10 Jckrs tranbefore to Nue of Eades Line											
10/15 Bulk	3/1	11	11	1110	1125		1124		1125	11.10	1110	1125	1135	
1/20 Uln	3/1	1258	1258	1259	1.14	1.13		1.14	1.11	1.11	114	120		
			M.F. Greaves on duty 1145 pm											
K Gds			3/05	39	54	51		56	3/0	3/0	56	3/10		Jan	
B. Bo Oil			3/05	3/10	17	17		18	3/10	3/10	18	28			
Bx To Bk		3/58 Back Cancelled						Going to work 3/1578						
On Eng out No 4 line								Ros Leto 4/5						
					Ms To Steps						High 14/5			
G.P Eng.			1417	25	39				1458	39	417			
B. 15?? Oil	6/11	17	26		28		29		16/11	26	39	X		
C 4/3 Pockes	1958	34	417						9/34	417	55			

Table 64

Passenger timetable for Winter 1957/8

Table 64

DIDCOT, NEWBURY, WINCHESTER and SOUTHAMPTON

WEEK DAYS ONLY

Mls		am	am		am		am		am	am	pm (TC Newbury to Bournemouth Cen. (arr 5 2 pm))	pm (Saturdays only)			pm (TC from Oxford)	pm		pm	
	152 Oxford .... dep		7 10				9 55			11 45		1 25			2 56	5 0			
—	**Didcot** .. .. .. dep		**7 40**				**10 50**			**12p42**		**2 0**			**3 38**	**5 55**			
3	Upton and Blewbury		7 47				10 58			12 49		2 7			3 45	6 2			
6¾	Churn		7 54				Aa			Aa		Aa			Aa	Aa			
8½	Compton		7 59				11 11			1 0		2 18			3 56	6 14			
10½	Hampstead Norris		8 4				11 17			1 5		2 25			4 1	6 20			
12¾	Pinewood Halt		8 10				11 23			1 11		2 31			4 7	6 27			
13½	Hermitage		8 13				11 27			1 14		2 34			4 10	6 32			
18	**Newbury** .... arr		**8 21**				**11 36**			**1 25**		**2 45**			**4 20**	**6 41**			
—	**62 London** (Pad.) .. dep				7H30				**10 18**		**12 30**				2 35			**6 0**	
—	**Newbury** .... dep	**7 45**			**9 7**				**12 25**		**2 0**				**4 32**			**7 25**	
21¼	Woodhay	7 52			9 15				12 32		2 7				4 39			7 32	
23½	Highclere	7 58			9 21				12 38		2 13				4 45			7 38	
25½	Burghclere	8 3			9 26				12 43		2 18				4 49			7 42	
28	Litchfield	8 10			9 32				12 49		2 24				4 55			7 49	
31¼	Whitchurch Town	8 18			9 40				12 56		2 32				5 3			7 56	
37¼	Sutton Scotney	8 29			9 51				1 7		2 43				5 14			8 7	
40¼	Worthy Down Halt	8 39			9 58				1 14		2 57				5 21			8 14	
42½	King's Worthy	8 44			10 3				1 19		3 2				5 25			8 18	
44¼	**Winchester Chesil** arr	**8 49**			**10 8**				**1 24**		**3 6**				**5 31**			**8 23**	
	Winchester Chesil dep	**8 51**			**10 9**				**1 25**		**3 7**				**5 32**			**8 24**	
47½	Shawford arr																		
51	Eastleigh "	9 3			10 22				1 37		3 18				5 44			8 37	
53½	Swaythling "	9 15			10X37														
54¾	St. Denys "	9 19			10X41						3 32								
55¾	Northam "	9 23			10X44														
56½	**Southampton Term.** ..	**9 26**			**10X47**														
56¾	**Southampton Cen.** .. arr										**3 38**								

Miles		am		am (TC Totton (dep 6 28 am) to Reading General; Reading Gen. arr 9 7 am)		am		am		am		pm		pm		pm		pm (Saturdays only)		pm	pm
	Southampton Cen. .. dep			**6 40**																	
	Southampton Term. dep									**11X50**										**4Z53**	
¾	Northam									11X53										4Z56	
1¾	St. Denys			6 46						11X57										5Z 0	
3¼	Swaythling			6 50						12X 1										5Z 4	
5½	Eastleigh			6 57		7 55		10 18		12 8				2 12						5 12	
9¼	Shawford			7 4		8 2		10 25		12 15				2 19						5 19	
12¾	**Winchester Chesil** arr			**7 12**		**8 10**		**10 34**		**12 23**				**2 27**						**5 27**	
	Winchester Chesil dep			**7 14**		**8 11**		**10 37**		**12 25**				**2 28**						**5 32**	
14	King's Worthy			7 20		8 16		10 44		12 31				2 34						5 39	
16½	Worthy Down Halt			7 26		8 22		10 50		12 37				2 40						5 45	
19	Sutton Scotney			7 33		8 30		10 56		12 44				2 48						5B54	
24¾	Whitchurch Town			7 45		8 41		11 7		12 55				3G 2						6B 7	
28½	Litchfield			7 54		8 50		11 16		1 7				3 12						6 16	
31	Burghclere			8C 4		8 56		11 22		1 13				3 18						6 23	
33	Highclere			8 11		9 1		11 26		1 17				3 20						6 28	
35¼	Woodhay			8 17		9 7		11 32		1 23				3 29						6 33	
38½	**Newbury** .. .. .. arr			**8 25**		**9 15**		**11 40**		**1 30**				**3 36**						**6 41**	
91½	**62 London** (Pad.) ... arr			**10 7**		**11 15**		**1 15**		**3 20**				**5V55**						**8 30**	
—	**Newbury** .. .. .. dep	**6 45**				**9 20**						**1 58**				**4 20**		**5 45**			**7 21**
43	Hermitage	6 55				9 30						2 7				4 29		5 54			7 30
43¾	Pinewood Halt	6 58				9 33						2 10				4 32		5 57			7 33
46	Hampstead Norris	7 3				9 39						2 16				4 38		6 3			7 39
48	Compton	7 12				9 45						2 21				4 44		6 9			7 44
49¾	Churn					Kk						Kk				Kk		Kk			Kk
53½	Upton and Blewbury	7 22				9 59						2 32				4 55		6 19			7 54
56½	**Didcot** .... arr	**7 28**				**10 5**						**2 38**				**5 4**		**6 25**			8 [illegible]
66½	152 Oxford .. .. arr	8 23				10 45						3 13				5 44		6 55			9H14

Aa Stops to take up or set down on previous notice to Station Master at Didcot. Evening trains call during daylight only
B Arr 2 minutes *earlier*
C Arr 4 minutes *earlier*
G Arr 5 minutes *earlier*
H On Saturdays arr 9 9 pm
Kk Stops to take up or set down on previous notice to Station Master at Newbury. Evening trains call during daylight only

H Second class only for a portion of the journey
p pm
TC Through Carriages
V On Saturdays second class only for a portion of the journey
X Until 2nd November, 1957, inclusive only
Z Weekdays until 2nd November, 1957, and Except Saturdays commencing 4th November, 1957

On Sundays, Bus services depart Didcot Station 3 0 pm to Newbury Station; returning from Newbury Station at 7 55 pm by Newbury and District Motor Services Ltd. Passengers holding rail tickets to or from Stations between Didcot and Newbury inclusive may travel by these Road services without additional charge